Second Grade

Everyday
Mathematics®

Assessment Handbook

Second Grade

Everyday Mathematics®

Assessment Handbook

The University of Chicago
School Mathematics Project

 Wright Group

The McGraw·Hill Companies

UCSMP Elementary Materials Component

Max Bell, Director

Authors

Jean Bell

William M. Carroll

Acknowledgments

We gratefully acknowledge the work of the following classroom teachers who provided input and suggestions as we designed this handbook: Huong Banh, Fran Moore, Jenny Waters, and Lana Winnet.

Photo Credits

Page 1, Michael Goss/Photography
Page 8, Phil Martin/Photography
Page 41, Phil Martin/Photography
Cover: Bill Burlingham/Photography
Photo Collage: Herman Adler Design

Contributors

Ellen Dairyko, Sharon Draznin, Nancy Hanvey, Laurie Leff, Denise Porter
Herb Price, Joyce Timmons, Lisa Winters

Wright Group

Send all inquiries to:
Wright Group/McGraw-Hill
P.O. Box 812960
Chicago, IL 60681

Printed in the United States of America.

ISBN 0-07-584468-0

8 9 10 11 12 POH 09 08 07 06 05

Contents

Introduction

Too often, school assessment is equated with testing and grading. While some formal assessment is necessary, it tends to provide only scattered snapshots of children rather than records of their growth and progress. The philosophy of *Everyday Mathematics*® is that real assessment should be more like a motion picture, revealing the development of the child's mathematical understanding while giving the teacher useful feedback about instructional needs. Rather than simply providing tests on isolated skills, *Everyday Mathematics* offers a variety of useful techniques and opportunities to assess children's progress on skills, concepts, and thinking processes.

Several assessment tools are built into the *Everyday Mathematics* program. Slate assessments and end-of-unit written assessments are useful in showing how well students are learning the concepts and skills covered in a unit. But these tools by themselves do not provide a balance, highlight progress, or show children's work on larger problems. The purpose of this handbook is to broaden your assessment techniques. Rather than using all of the techniques suggested here, choose a few that balance written work with observation, individual work with group work, and short answers with longer explanations.

For assessment to be valid and useful to both teachers and children, the authors believe that

- teachers need to have a variety of assessment tools and techniques from which to choose.
- children should be included in the assessment process through interviews, written work, and conferences that provide appropriate feedback. Self-assessment and reflection are skills that will develop over time if encouraged.
- assessment and instruction should be closely linked. Assessment should assist teachers in making instructional decisions concerning both individual children and the whole class.
- a good assessment plan makes instruction easier.
- the best assessment plans are those developed by teachers working collaboratively within their schools.

This handbook compiles classroom-tested techniques used by experienced *Everyday Mathematics* teachers. It includes suggestions for observing students, keeping anecdotal records, following student progress, and encouraging children to reflect on and communicate both what they have learned and how they feel about mathematics. Many of the assessment suggestions are aimed specifically at *Everyday Mathematics* activities, such as using Explorations to observe students or using Math Boxes to focus on a particular concept or skill.

As you read through this handbook, you may want to start with one or two activities that fit your needs and assist you in building a balanced approach to assessment. Feel free to adapt the materials to your own needs. While some teachers find Math Logs useful, others find observations and short, informal interviews more helpful.

The *Everyday Mathematics* goal is to furnish you with some ideas to make assessment and instruction more manageable, productive, and exciting as well as offer you a more complete picture of each child's progress and instructional needs.

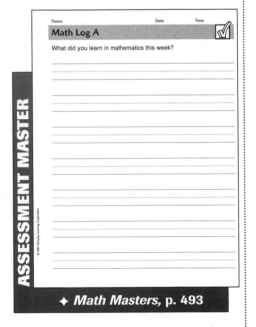

◆ *Math Masters, p. 493*

ASSESSMENT MASTER

A Balance of Assessments

Although there is no one "right" assessment plan for all classrooms, all assessment plans should use a variety of techniques. To develop your own plan, consider four different assessment sources within the Quad shown in the figure below. The content of this handbook provides further details about these sources. The section beginning on page 39 provides examples for each unit of how to use different types of assessments in specific lessons.

Ongoing, Product, and Periodic Assessments, and Outside Tests

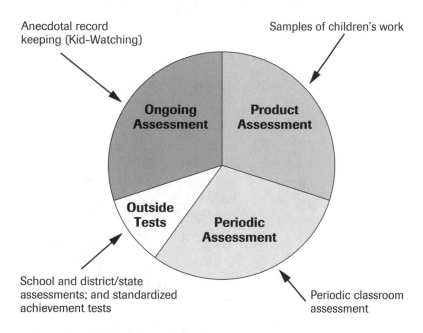

Anecdotal record keeping (Kid-Watching)

Samples of children's work

Ongoing Assessment

Product Assessment

Outside Tests

Periodic Assessment

School and district/state assessments; and standardized achievement tests

Periodic classroom assessment

Ongoing Assessment includes observations of children as they are working on regular classroom activities, in groups during Explorations and games, or independently on Math Boxes. It also may include children's thinking and shared strategies as well as information you gather from classroom interactions or brief, informal, individual interviews. Records of these ongoing assessments may take the form of short written notes, more elaborate record sheets, or brief mental notes to yourself. See Ongoing Assessment, pages 13–17, for details.

Product Assessment may include samples of daily written work; group project reports; and mathematical writing, drawing, sketches, diagrams, or anything else you feel has value and reflects what you want children to learn. If you are keeping portfolios, children should help select which products to include in them. See Portfolios, pages 7–10, and Product Assessment, pages 19–23.

Periodic Assessment includes more formal assessments, such as end-of-unit assessments, quizzes, Progress Indicators, and Math Interest Inventories. Pages 25–33 offer suggestions and extensions intended to help you measure both individual and class progress using these types of assessment.

Outside Tests provide information from school, district, state, or standardized tests that might be used to evaluate the progress of a child, class, or school. See pages 35 and 36 for more information.

The types of assessment sources used within the Quad are quite flexible and depend on a number of factors, such as grade level, children's experience, time of year, and so on. For example, Kindergarten and first grade teachers, especially at the beginning of the year, probably use more of the material from the Ongoing Assessment source and less from Product and Periodic Assessment sources. In contrast, teachers in higher grades may rely more on the Product, Periodic, and Outside Assessment sources.

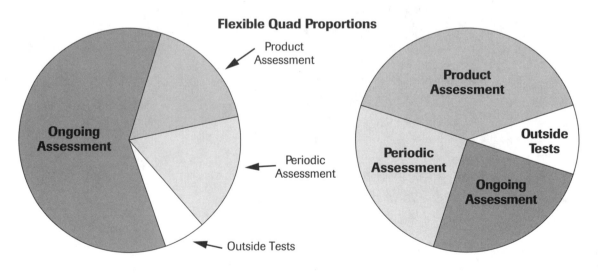

Flexible Quad Proportions

Product Assessment

Ongoing Assessment

Periodic Assessment

Outside Tests

Possible First Grade Proportions

Product Assessment

Outside Tests

Periodic Assessment

Ongoing Assessment

Possible Second Grade Proportions

A List of Assessment Sources attached to children's folders or portfolios or kept in your record book may help you see whether you have included information from the first three sources of the Quad as well as from other sources. Notice that the completed sample shown below includes only a few of the assessment suggestions from each source. Another teacher might choose other entries. Using multiple techniques will give you a clear picture of each child's progress and instructional needs.

Use this List of Assessment Sources master to keep track of the assessment sources that you are currently using. A blank sample is provided in *Math Masters,* page 484. The Assessment Masters, included at the back of your *Math Masters* book, are shown in reduced form on pages 82–122 of this book.

NOTE: Do not try to use all assessment sources at once. Instead, devise a manageable, balanced plan.

Your assessment plan should answer these questions:
- *How is the class performing as a whole?*
- *How are individual children performing?*
- *How can I adjust instruction to meet children's needs?*
- *How can I communicate to children, parents, and others about the progress being made?*

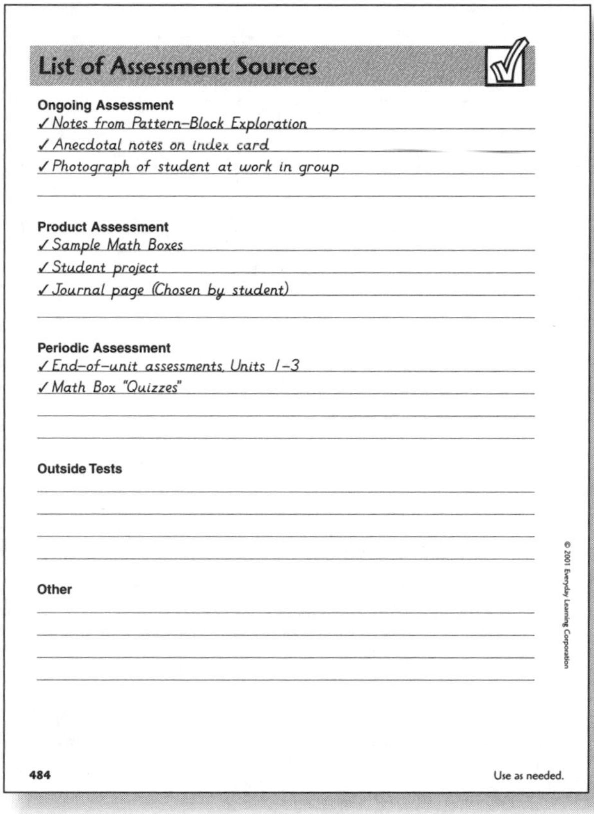

List of Assessment Sources

Ongoing Assessment
✓ Notes from Pattern–Block Exploration
✓ Anecdotal notes on index card
✓ Photograph of student at work in group

Product Assessment
✓ Sample Math Boxes
✓ Student project
✓ Journal page (Chosen by student)

Periodic Assessment
✓ End–of–unit assessments, Units 1–3
✓ Math Box "Quizzes"

Outside Tests

Other

484   Use as needed.

© 2001 Everyday Learning Corporation

Your Assessment Ideas

Portfolios

Using Portfolios

Portfolios are used for a number of different purposes, from keeping track of progress to helping children become more reflective about their mathematical growth. Because many schools, districts, and states are developing their own guidelines and requirements for portfolios, the *Everyday Mathematics* authors are reluctant to make specific suggestions. However, there are several reasons that the practice of keeping portfolios is positive and consistent with the philosophy of *Everyday Mathematics*:

• Portfolios emphasize progress over time, rather than results at a given moment. At any time, a child may have Beginning, Developing, or Secure understandings of various mathematical concepts. This progress can best be exhibited by a collection of products organized into portfolios or folders that contain work from different contexts and from different times in the year.

• Portfolios can involve children more directly in the assessment process. Children may write introductions and help select portfolio entries. They can select work they are especially proud of and tag each piece with an explanation of why it was chosen. The margin sample shows how a child might use self-assessment forms to tag and evaluate a piece of work. Children may need guidance in developing realistic self-assessment, which is a valuable skill that takes time to develop. Blank self-assessment forms (My Work) are provided in *Math Masters*, pages 496 and 497.

• Portfolios can be used as evidence of progress for children, their families, and their teachers for next year. You may want to establish a "Portfolio Night" for children and their parents to attend in order to allow them time to discuss and review the contents. It is very important that parents understand the goals of certain projects and assignments.

• Portfolios can illustrate children's strengths and weaknesses in particular areas of mathematics. Since a rich body of work can be contained in a portfolio, it is a good vehicle for exhibiting each child's progress. It also can be used to assess children's abilities to see connections within mathematics and to apply mathematical ideas to real-world situations.

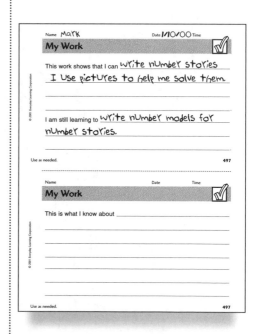

Some teachers keep two types of portfolios: a working portfolio in which students store their recent work and an assessment portfolio. Occasionally, a selection of work is transferred from the working portfolio to the assessment portfolio. Usually, the teacher provides some guidelines for what should be selected, allowing children to choose within these guidelines.

Many teachers recommend that the number of mathematics entries in an assessment portfolio be kept to a limited number. These entries provide a manageable but representative sample of work. New work can replace old, but some samples from throughout the year should remain.

Listed below are some ideas of representative work that might be included in a portfolio:

• Projects in progress and in completed form

• Children's solutions to challenging problems

• Written accounts of children's feelings about mathematics

• Drawings, sketches, and representations of mathematical ideas and situations

• Photographs of children interacting with manipulatives

• Photographs of children working individually and in groups

• Videos portraying children communicating mathematically

For more guidance on developing portfolio assessment, you may wish to consult one of several excellent sources listed on page 37 of this handbook. We especially recommend *Mathematics Assessment: Myths, Models, Good Questions, and Practical Suggestions,* edited by Jean Kerr Stenmark, available through the National Council of Teachers of Mathematics (NCTM). Portfolios, as well as other assessment issues, are also frequently addressed in the NCTM journal *Teaching Children Mathematics.* A video available from NCTM, *Mathematics Assessment: Alternative Approaches,* also discusses portfolios and may be helpful for teachers who are working together to develop a schoolwide assessment policy.

Ideas in the *Teacher's Lesson Guide*

Portfolio Ideas Samples of children's work may be obtained from the following assignments:

Unit 1
- Using Tally Marks to Record Survey Responses (**Lesson 1.5**)
- Making Individual Number Scrolls (**Lesson 1.8**)
- Create Number-Grid Puzzles (**Lesson 1.14**)

Unit 2
- Making Up Addition Number Stories for a Bulletin Board or Book (**Lesson 2.1**)
- Creating and Solving Riddles (**Lesson 2.4**)
- Write and Solve Addition and Subtraction Number Stories (**Lesson 2.14**)

Unit 3
- Making a Clock Booklet (**Lesson 3.4**)

Unit 4
- Making Coin-Stamp Booklets (**Lesson 4.3**)
- Exploring Pattern-Block Designs (**Lesson 4.9**)

Unit 5
- Exploring Equal Sharing (**Lesson 5.2**)
- Making Centimeter-Cube Arrays (**Lesson 5.3**)
- Making a Dollar (**Lesson 5.3**)
- Creating a Booklet or Bulletin-Board Display of Parallel Line Segments (**Lesson 5.5**)
- Making Shapes out of Triangles and Rectangles (**Lesson 5.6**)
- Making a Symmetry Booklet (**Lesson 5.9**)
- Make Symmetrical Shapes (**Lesson 5.10**)

Unit 6

- Favorite-Food Data **(Lesson 6.3)**
- Number Stories **(Lesson 6.4)**
- Subtraction Number Stories **(Lesson 6.6)**
- Creating Pattern-Block Symmetry **(Lesson 6.7)**
- Describe a Method Used to Solve a Multidigit Subtraction Problem **(Lesson 6.12)**
- Make Up and Solve Number Stories Involving Addition, Subtraction, Equal Groups, Equal Sharing, or Equal Grouping **(Lesson 6.12)**

Unit 7

- Making Patterns by Coloring Grids **(Lesson 7.1)**
- Making Up Arrow-Path Puzzles **(Lesson 7.2)**
- Making Up and Solving Number Stories **(Lesson 7.7)**
- Write a Doubles or Halves Story **(Lesson 7.10)**

Unit 8

- Making a Collection of "Collective Terms" **(Lesson 8.3)**
- Making Books of Fraction Number Stories **(Lesson 8.7)**
- Name Fractional Parts of a Region **(Lesson 8.8)**
- Describe Fractions Greater Than ONE **(Lesson 8.8)**
- Write and Solve Number Stories Involving Fractions **(Lesson 8.8)**

Unit 9

- Solving Road-Map Stories **(Lesson 9.5)**
- Researching a Pretend Trip **(Lesson 9.5)**
- Making a Measuring Tools Booklet **(Lesson 9.6)**
- Finding the Areas of Grid-Paper Drawings **(Lesson 9.8)**

Unit 10

- Write about Mathematics **(Lesson 10.12)**
- Write Number Stories **(Lesson 10.12)**

Unit 11

- Making Up and Solving Number Stories about Purchases **(Lesson 11.1)**
- Making Up and Solving Multiplication and Division Number Stories **(Lesson 11.7)**
- Write about Mathematics **(Lesson 11.10)**
- Make Up and Solve Addition, Subtraction, Multiplication, and Division Number Stories **(Lesson 11.10)**

Unit 12

- Creating a Timeline of a Person's Life **(Lesson 12.3)**
- Connecting Comparisons of Animal Speeds to Literature **(Lesson 12.6)**
- Collecting and Displaying Class Height Data **(Lesson 12.7)**

POD of WhAIes

Rubrics

One good way to keep track of each child's progress is to use a rubric. A rubric is a framework that helps you categorize progress on various aspects of a child's learning. A simple but effective rubric that many teachers use is the classification of children as Beginning, Developing, or Secure with respect to a particular skill or concept. This is illustrated below.

Sample Rubric
Beginning (B)   Children cannot complete the task independently. They show little understanding of the concept or skill.
Developing (D)   Children show some understanding. However, errors or misunderstandings still occur. Reminders, hints, and suggestions are needed to promote children's understanding.
Secure (S)   Children can apply the skill or concept correctly and independently.

This simple rubric can be easily used with any of the sample assessment tools to keep track of the progress of individual children as well as the whole class. You may wish to use B, D, and S or another set of symbols, such as –, ✓, and +; Levels C, B, and A; or some other rubric symbols you prefer. One teacher suggests using red, yellow, and green color symbols.

No matter which rubric symbols you use, you can take a quick look at a completed Class Checklist or a Class Progress Indicator to see which areas need further review or which children will benefit from additional help or challenge.

Because some children fall between Developing and Secure or may show exemplary understanding, a 3-point rubric may seem insufficient for some areas you wish to assess. This may be especially true when you are examining performance on a Project or other larger activity. A general five-level rubric follows on the next page.

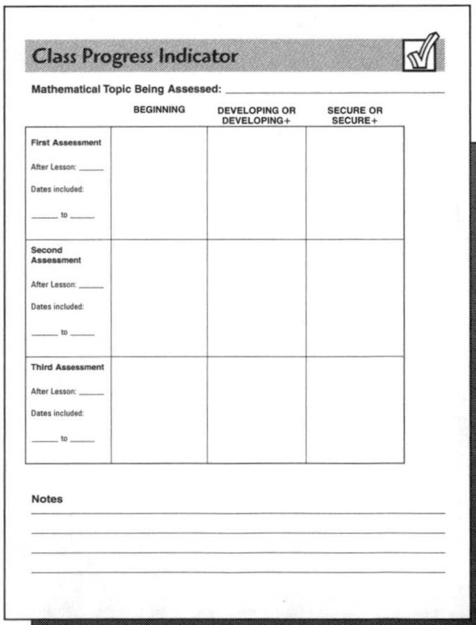

Class Progress Indicator

Mathematical Topic Being Assessed: _____

	BEGINNING	DEVELOPING OR DEVELOPING+	SECURE OR SECURE+
First Assessment After Lesson: _____ Dates included: _____ to _____			
Second Assessment After Lesson: _____ Dates included: _____ to _____			
Third Assessment After Lesson: _____ Dates included: _____ to _____			

Notes

_____
_____
_____

ASSESSMENT MASTER

◆ *Math Masters,* **p. 488**

Remember, the rubrics are only a framework. When you wish to use a rubric, general indicators should be made more specific to fit the task, the time of the year, and the grade level at which the rubric is being used. Some examples of rubrics applied to specific tasks are illustrated in this book in the section on Progress Indicators/Performance Indicators beginning on page 27.

Finally, another example of a general rubric is given below. This rubric might be applied to a problem in which children are asked both to find an answer and to explain (or illustrate) their reasoning. Rubrics like these can be used to assess not only individual performance on an extended problem, but also group processes on problem-solving tasks.

Sample Rubric

Level 0
No attempts are made to solve the problem.

Level 1
Partial attempts are made. Reasoning is not explained. Problems are misunderstood, or little progress is made.

Level 2
Children arrive at solutions, and children clearly show reasoning and correct processes, but solutions are incorrect.
or:
Solutions are correct with little or no explanation given.

Level 3
Solutions are correct. Explanations are attempted but are incomplete.

Level 4
Solutions are correct. Explanations are clear and complete.

Level 5
Children offer exemplary solutions.

Ongoing Assessment

Observation of children during regular classroom interactions, as they work independently or in groups, is an important assessment technique in *Everyday Mathematics*. The following suggestions may help you manage and record these ongoing observations.

Recording Tools

Flip-Card Collection

Some teachers have found it helpful to attach index cards to a clipboard for recording observations. To do this, use one card for each child. You can use one color for the first five children, a second color for the next five children, and so on. Focus on one set of five each day, along with any other anecdotal observations from the rest of the children. Try to observe each child at least once every two weeks. Be sure to date your observations so that you can track improvements.

After a child's index card has become filled with information, remove it and file it alphabetically. Tape a new card to the clipboard to repeat the process.

The completed cards will help you keep track of children's needs and the implications for instruction. They are also useful for preparing for parent conferences.

Seating Charts or Calendar Grids

Place each child's name in one of the grid cells and write observations in the cells as you circulate throughout the classroom. After reflecting on whole-class needs, cut apart the cells, date them, and file them for each child. Use them to analyze individual strengths and needs and to prepare for parent conferences.

Computer Labels

Print out children's names on sheets of large computer address labels. Write observations on the appropriate labels. As labels become filled, place them on cards or in a notebook for individual children.

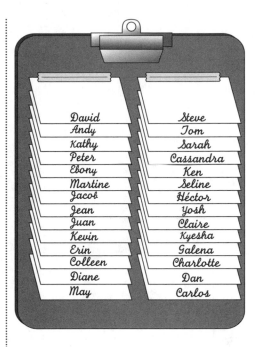

NOTE: Sequentially number the reviewed cards for each child so that you can easily see children who may have been missed (for example, you might notice that you are on Card #3 for most of the children and still on Card #1 for a few).

Observational Class Checklists

A blank checklist is provided on *Math Masters,* page 486. You may want to use it for recording ongoing observations and interactions.

So that you won't have to rewrite children's names on each checklist you use, make a copy of the blank checklist. On the copy, list the names of your children, perhaps by the groups you wish to assess at any one time. This will be your "Class Checklist" from which additional copies can be made. List the learning goals you are currently teaching and wish to assess.

The blank "Names" Master (*Math Masters,* page 487) is provided so that, if necessary, you can change the order of children's names on subsequent "Class Checklists" or on any of the grade-level checklists referred to in this handbook.

One teacher suggests attaching a blank Class Checklist to the back of a flip-card clipboard or a similar ongoing recording device and then identifying a particular concept or skill and using a rubric symbol on the checklist to indicate students' progress. (See information on Rubrics, pages 11 and 12.) Blank cells can show which children to focus on the next time you revisit the topic. The checklist indicates which children or which topics should require additional attention.

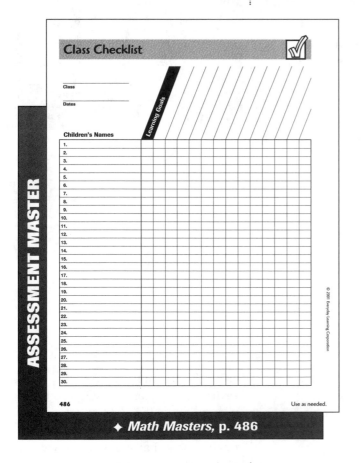

♦ *Math Masters,* p. 486

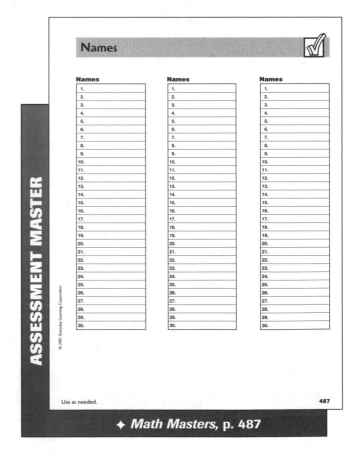

♦ *Math Masters,* p. 487

Math Box Cover-Up

Some teachers use Math Boxes to assess progress. The scenario below is from an *Everyday Mathematics* teacher.

One Teacher's Use of Math Boxes

Much of the assessment in Ms. Summers' third grade classroom is ongoing observation—short notes on progress made as children work on an activity. Generally, children are unaware that they are being assessed. For example, as children are working on a set of Math Boxes, Ms. Summers has a copy of the day's Math Boxes page attached to her clipboard and has identified particular cells that she would like to assess. These identified cells are covered with self-stick notes.

As she circulates through the classroom, Ms. Summers observes children's performance on these targeted cells. If a child is having difficulty with a particular cell, Ms. Summers may ask a probing question or two. If appropriate, the child's name is recorded on that self-stick note, sometimes with a note about the particular difficulty the child seems to be having.

Ms. Summers may also indicate the progress that she sees various children making, as well as the names of those who need extended challenges.

Later, Ms. Summers works with those children who need additional review, either individually or in a small group.

In sum, Ms. Summers uses Math Boxes to reinforce, review, and extend particular skills and concepts. If a particular concept is troublesome for the class, it will be revisited in future lessons and Math Boxes.

Ms. Summers also uses Math Boxes to communicate with parents and guardians about the mathematics being taught in the classroom and about individual children's strengths and weaknesses. Along with her observational notes, Ms. Summers finds Math Boxes to be a useful tool for assessing the progress both of her class and of individual children.

Using Recording Tools

Finding time to use the recording tools suggested in the previous section is important. Choose the one that appeals to you most and try it. If necessary, adapt it to make it more useful to you, or try another tool. Listed below are some *Everyday Mathematics* approaches and routines, with suggestions on ways to use recording tools.

Teacher-Guided Instruction

During the lesson, circulate around the room, interacting with children and observing the mathematical behavior that is taking place. Identify those children who are having difficulty as well as those who are showing progress. Be alert to significant comments and interactions. These quick observations often tell a great deal about a child's mathematical thinking. Practice making mental notes on the spot, and follow them up with brief written notes when possible. The important thing is to find an efficient way to keep track of children's progress without getting overwhelmed with papers, lists, and notes.

Mathematical Mini-Interviews

Observing and listening to children as they work will enable you to note progress. However, there are times when brief oral interactions with probing questions clarify and enhance observations. These brief, nonthreatening, one-on-one interactions overheard by the rest of the class or in private, as appropriate, encourage mathematical communication skills. They should, however, apply to the content at hand. For example, when children are counting as a group, you may ask some of them, "Let's see how high you can count by 3s." Or, when second graders are explaining addition strategies, you might ask, "What does the 2 in 427 mean?" or "What are the units for this number story?"

Games

At the beginning of the year, when children are first becoming comfortable with the games and are playing them in small groups, move around the classroom observing the strategies that children are employing. Once children are playing the games independently, assemble a small group of those having difficulty with Math Boxes cells, computational strategies, or other related problem areas and provide help. Use the recording tools to note any valuable information regarding individual mathematical development. You can also use this time to conduct mathematical mini-interviews.

Mental Math and Reflexes

As you present the class with Mental Math and Reflexes situations, focus on a small core group of children. For example, you might start with the first five children on the clipboard or grid. You should never feel that all children need to be observed every day.

Strategy Sharing

Over time, encourage each child to share his or her strategies while working at the board or overhead projector. It is during this time that you should assume the role of "guide on the side" rather than "sage on the stage." Record which strategies the child uses. In the *Everyday Mathematics* classroom, many strategies are being utilized; recording children's strategies will help you know how to address individual strengths and needs. You will also have an opportunity to consider communication skills and processes as well as answers.

Explorations

During Explorations lessons, you can observe children participating in manipulative-based activities. As children work in small groups, you may wish to observe specific children. Another option is to establish your own workstation. As you guide children through an Exploration, note the processes, the verbalization, and the thinking that are taking place.

Slates

Periodically, record children's responses from their slate reviews. You may want to focus on one group at a time and indicate only those children with Beginning understanding. Provide follow-up instruction for them based on your notes.

Your Assessment Ideas

_____

_____

_____

_____

_____

_____

_____

_____

_____

_____

_____

_____

_____

_____

_____

_____

_____

_____

_____

_____

_____

_____

_____

_____

_____

_____

_____

Your Assessment Ideas

Product Assessment

Samples of children's mathematical writings, drawing, and creations add breadth to the assessment process. In this section, the *Everyday Mathematics* authors offer suggestions and other sources for product assessment and review some of the products that are part of *Everyday Mathematics*. Some of these items can be selected and stored in a portfolio or work folder along with other assessments.

Products from *Everyday Mathematics*

Math Boxes

Math Boxes provide quick glimpses into how a child performs in several areas. As suggested in the Ongoing Assessment section of this book, they can also be adapted to assess topics of concern. You may find it useful to check two or three specific items that repeat throughout the year, such as Frames and Arrows or "What's My Rule?" tables.

Math Journals

Math Journals can be considered working portfolios. Children should keep the journals intact so that they can revisit, review, correct, and improve their responses at a later time. You or children might select journal pages focusing on topics of concern or number stories featuring "do your own" exercises to photocopy and include in portfolios.

Math Masters

Math Masters, such as Home Links, may be collected or copied (in the case of the personal data pages) and used for product assessment. Although Home Links are less useful for assessing children because of home differences, they *can* be used to initiate discussion at parent conferences. Some teachers work on the Home Links with children in class and then send them home for discussion.

Explorations and Projects

Some of the Explorations and Projects generate 3-dimensional products that are either transitional or permanent. Displays, the use of a Polaroid camera, or brief videos can be helpful in capturing some of these products.

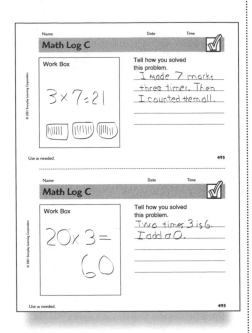

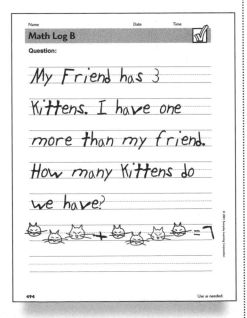

Additional Assessment Products

Many teachers are interested in gathering examples of children's writing and thinking in addition to those provided by *Everyday Mathematics* materials. This type of writing is usually more open-ended and provides children with opportunities to reflect, assess their understanding, and enhance their communication skills. This section offers examples of products you may want to include in your assessment plan.

Math Logs and Alternatives

Some teachers find it beneficial for children to write about mathematics regularly. A spiral notebook or a set of log sheets can be used as a Math Log. (See sample masters on *Math Masters,* pages 493–495.) Children may use the back side of Math Log sheets to draw a picture to illustrate what they learned. Not only can these written reflections serve as a powerful means of checking children's understanding, but they are also a means of assessing curiosity, persistence, and self-confidence.

Remember that Math Logs are not "end products" but, instead, are an important part of the ongoing assessment process referred to on page 3. They are helpful to both you and children only if they reveal useful information and encourage the development of mathematical thinking, understanding, and written communication. Here are some suggestions on how to get children writing:

Open-Ended Questions Use open-ended questions to start children writing. Some prompts that you can use are:

• *Why is (this answer) right or wrong? Explain.*

• *What was your strategy for finding the answer?*

• *How many ways can you find an answer for this problem?*

• *How is this like something you have learned before?*

Children may use My Exit Slip sheets to record responses to open-ended questions at the close of a lesson or unit. (See *Math Masters,* page 498.)

Number Stories Occasionally ask children to write and/or draw a number story. Sometimes, you may wish to supply the numbers. For example:

• *Write a number story that uses the numbers 8 and 5.*

At other times, you may leave the instructions more open-ended:

• *Make up a number story using large numbers.*

• *Write or draw a number story that shows addition.*

Written number stories provide concrete assessment of children's understanding of operations, relationships, and numbers. For example, many children confuse addition situations with subtraction situations. Number stories often point out misconceptions.

Portfolio Writing If you are using portfolios, children can write or dictate entries for their portfolios to show what they know about numbers and mathematics. Children might dictate their ideas to you or to a classroom aide. Provide prompts like the following to encourage children to show what they already know:

• *What do you hope to learn about mathematics this year?*

• *Why is mathematics important?*

As the year continues and entries change, ask children to update their introductions and include short descriptions of the different pieces. At the end of the year, children can make a list of important things that they learned.

Concept and Strategy Writing Prior to the teaching of a unit, invite children to share what they already know about the concepts being presented. For example, before you teach a unit on multiplication, children could reflect in response to the following prompts:

• *Show me any multiplication that you can do.*

• *What is multiplication?*

• *Explain the strategy you used to solve the problem.*

• *Explain your thinking.*

Children's reflections may help you plan your instruction. At the close of each unit, ask children to respond to the same statements or questions. This allows both you and the children to compare growth in understanding of the concepts.

Later in the year, children can begin to use words, pictures, or both to explain strategies they used to solve problems. Communicating about mathematics encourages children to reflect upon their thinking and provides you with another perspective on the strategies children use. Ask a question and encourage children to write ways for solving the problem. Model this for the children.

If you do not want to have children keep regular Math Logs, ask them to occasionally write about mathematics so that they can develop this skill. Once every unit, give children short writing assignments. Ideas can come from any of the Math Log suggestions mentioned previously in this section. These can be given as a Math Message or as part of a Math Boxes assignment. They can be short reflections written just before the end-of-unit assessment. For example:

• *The math I know best / least in this unit is _____.*

They could also be more content-oriented assignments. For example:

• *Look around the room and find two geometric shapes. Draw them and write a few sentences about them.*

6×5
This is easy because I know that $6 \times 10 = 60$ but 6×5 is half of this because 2 fives is 10. So I get 30.

My Math Strategies

$$\begin{array}{r} 26 \\ + 78 \\ \hline 90 \\ + 14 \\ \hline 104 \end{array}$$

I started with the tens place and added $70 + 20$ which was 90. So then I went over to the ones place and added $6 + 8$ which was 14. So then I added them together and a total $90 + 14 = 104$.

NOTE: Do not feel discouraged if children have difficulty communicating mathematically. This is a skill that takes time to develop.

Children who begin the year having nothing to say or who answer in short, incomplete sentences become much more fluent as the year progresses.

How often should you use a Math Log or other writing in your math program? This depends on you and your children. While some teachers use logs a few times per week, you may find that once a week (perhaps on Friday, reflecting on what children did that week) or at the end of the unit is sufficient.

Choose the amount of additional writing with which you and your children feel comfortable.

Children's Reflections and Self-Assessment

Try to include children in the assessment process. The products listed below will encourage children to develop their ability to think reflectively. These products can be used as Math Messages or Home Links within the program, in Math Logs, or as alternatives to Math Logs.

Open-ended questions, such as those suggested below, provide children with opportunities to reflect on what they know and what they do not know. Invite children to reflect before, during, and/or after a lesson.

Math Masters, pages 493–498 provide alternative formats offered by experienced *Everyday Mathematics* teachers. "My Exit Slips" are suggested for responses to appropriate open-ended questions at the end of a lesson or a unit. Here are some prompts you can use:

- *My goal for tomorrow is...*
- *I learned that...*
- *I was surprised that I...*
- *I was pleased that I...*
- *I still don't understand...*
- *Because of the mathematics lesson today, I feel more confident about...*
- *The most important thing I learned in* Everyday Mathematics *today (this week) is...*
- *I think (fractions, calculators) are...*
- *(Subtraction) is easy if...*
- *The trouble with mathematics is...*
- *What I like most (or least) about* Everyday Mathematics *is...*

End-of-unit writing can help children practice self-reflection by focusing them on what they worked on during the unit.

- *In this unit, one new thing I learned is _____.*
- *One thing I still need to practice is _____.*
- *How would you explain to an absent student what we did today?*
- *What was the most difficult (easiest) part of today's lesson?*
- *Write a test problem that I might give to see if you understand today's lesson.*
- *What did you learn today that you did not know before?*
- *Tell me what you liked or disliked about today's lesson. Why?*

Sometimes you may want students to focus on how they worked in a small group:

- *What worked well in your group today?*
- *Describe what your job was in your group today.*
- *What could you have done to help your group work better?*
- *What do you like or dislike about working in a group?*

This kind of writing may give teachers some ideas about children's attitudes toward mathematics and about which experiences have been the most beneficial. Responses will vary, depending on the writing and reflective experiences of children.

> Sharing stratigies is fun because when you get up to the overhead it feels like you're the teacher.
>
> Math is fun when you're in 2nd grade. I hope I will improve in 3rd grade! Math is very fun!

Your Assessment Ideas

_____
_____
_____
_____
_____
_____
_____
_____
_____
_____
_____
_____
_____
_____
_____
_____
_____
_____
_____
_____
_____
_____
_____
_____
_____
_____

Periodic Assessment

Periodic assessment activities are those that are done at fairly consistent times or intervals over the school year. We will briefly review periodic assessment sources that are currently part of *Everyday Mathematics* and then discuss additional sources that experienced teachers use.

Sources from *Everyday Mathematics*

Unit Reviews and Assessments

Each unit of your Teacher's Lesson Guide ends with a review and assessment lesson that lists the learning goals for that unit. The goals list is followed by a cumulative review that includes suggestions for oral and slate assessments as well as a list of the written assessment items from the Checking Progress Assessment Masters for the unit. And each of these written assessment items is matched to one or more of the learning goals.

This cumulative oral, slate, and written review provides an opportunity for you to check children's progress on concepts and skills that were introduced or further developed in the unit.

Some additional reminders:

- Use rubrics to record children's progress toward each learning goal you assess. Rubrics are introduced on pages 11 and 12 of this book, and examples of how to use them are provided on pages 27–30 and in the Assessment Overview section beginning on page 39.

- Only concepts and skills that are the focus of several activities within any given unit are suggested for assessment at the end of a unit. However, feel free to add concepts and skills that you particularly want to assess or skills from previous units that you wish to reassess.

- Since many of the end-of-unit reviews and assessments tend to focus on skills, you may want to add more conceptual and open-ended questions as suggested in the Product Assessment section of this book, beginning on page 19.

> NOTE: If needed, generate your own reviews and quizzes for periodic review and assessment.
>
> Please give us feedback on your review and assessment ideas; this information may be beneficial to other teachers.

Math Boxes and Other *Math Journal* Pages

You can use rubrics to periodically assess Math Boxes and other *Math Journal* pages as independent reviews. By recording appropriate rubric symbols on a Class Progress Indicator (see page 27) or a Class Checklist, you can ascertain which children may need additional experience and perhaps pair or group them with children who offer Secure responses.

Midyear and End-of-Year Assessments

The Midyear and End-of-Year Assessment Masters (*Math Masters,* pages 438–447) provide additional assessment opportunities that you may wish to use as part of your balanced assessment plan. Minis of these masters, with answers, are shown on pages 91–96 of this book. These tests cover important concepts and skills presented in *Second Grade Everyday Mathematics,* but they are not designed to be used as "pre-tests" and they should not be your primary assessment tools. Use them along with the ongoing, product, and periodic assessments that are found within the lessons and at the end of each unit.

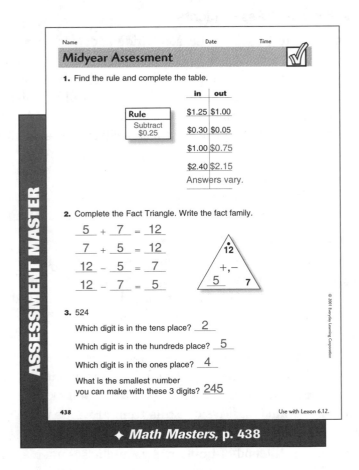

✦ *Math Masters,* p. 438

Additional Sources

Progress Indicators/Performance Indicators

Class Progress Indicators, also known as Performance Indicators, are another assessment tool that some teachers have found useful in assessing and tracking children's progress on selected mathematical topics. For example, early in second grade, you would expect most students to be Beginning or Developing when making change. However, by spring, many children will be Secure, and the rest should be Developing. Progress of the whole class, as well as individual children, can be assessed periodically, and appropriate instruction planned accordingly.

A Class Progress Indicator form provides space to record children's performance on any mathematical topic you choose to assess two or three times during the year.

The first assessment opportunity, usually after children have some exposure to and experience with a topic, provides a baseline for your children's performance early in the year. By recording the second and third assessments on the same form, you can track the progress of each child as well as the whole class throughout the school year. A second grade teacher's sample Class Progress Indicator for Making Change is shown below. A blank form of this master is provided in *Math Masters,* page 488.

Record the names of children under the columns that most appropriately indicate their levels: Beginning, Developing, or Secure (or whichever rubric symbols you want to use). If you wish, use a plus symbol (+) to indicate children who are between the given levels. As you conduct your assessments, keep this question in mind: *What do I need to do instructionally to promote progress?* Space is provided at the bottom of the form for any notes you may wish to make.

You may adapt the general rubric (Beginning, Developing, Developing+, Secure, Secure+) to your particular class level. On the pages that follow, we offer examples for two mathematical topics. For each of these topics, suggested assessment times are provided, along with specific rubrics. Use the rubric provided or feel free to adapt one to your own class. A blank rubric form is provided on page 490 of *Math Masters.* Use the Class Progress Indicator to assess other topics (such as Frames and Arrows, Numeration, and so on). However, do not assess more than two or three topics the first time through.

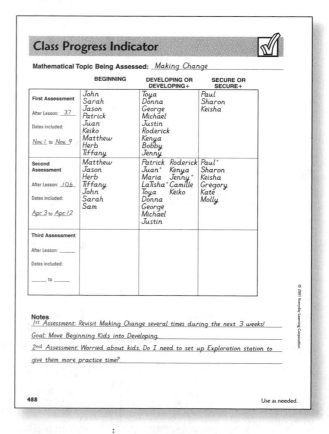

The teachers who prepared the following examples reported that creating these specific topic rubrics was not an easy task. Collaborating with colleagues proved helpful. The process takes time, but it becomes easier and is well worth the effort.

Example 1: Linear Measure

Linear measure begins in *Kindergarten Everyday Mathematics.* Measurement entails the use of tools, numeration, knowledge of units, and, later, knowledge of fractions and fractional notation. Because measuring is an active process, assessment should include observations of the measuring process along with a recorded answer.

Time Frame: Use during, with, or after Lessons 4.7 and 9.4.

Children work with linear measure in *Second Grade Everyday Mathematics* Exploration D in Lesson 4.7. You can use pages 100 and 101 in *Math Journal 1* for the baseline assessment (or make a copy so you can collect it).

Try to make this assessment performance-based. If possible, seat yourself at the station and take notes or use a rubric as children measure and record. (For example, "Jimmy has difficulty correctly lining up the end of the tape measure with the end of the object. But he is able to read the measurement scales correctly.") This kind of observation will provide more information about the source of errors (for example, incorrect use of tool, incorrect unit, or recording error).

The second assessment includes both linear measure and the concept of perimeter. You can conduct this assessment during or sometime after Lesson 9.4, using *Math Journal 2,* pages 148–151 (or a copy). Again, try to include observations of the children's errors.

Sample Linear-Measure Rubric

Sample Rubric

Beginning (B)
Children are unable to measure independently because of using the tool incorrectly or being unable to read or interpret the measure. There is little understanding of different linear units.

Developing (D)
Children may require some assistance in reading a measure. Some minor errors may occur, but in general, children understand the concept of linear measure.

Secure (S)
Children select and use tools independently. They can identify correct units of measure being used (inch, centimeter) and accurately measure and record the result. Children have a good sense of the reasonableness of a measure.

Two suggestions are provided for the last assessment on linear measure. You can use *Math Journal 2,* pages 152 and 153 (or a copy). Or children can draw shapes from their Pattern-Block Templates and measure them to the nearest inch or centimeter with *Math Masters,* page 499.

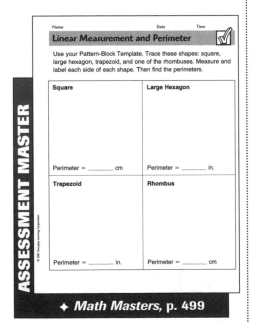

ASSESSMENT MASTER

Linear Measurement and Perimeter

Use your Pattern-Block Template. Trace these shapes: square, large hexagon, trapezoid, and one of the rhombuses. Measure and label each side of each shape. Then find the perimeters.

Square	Large Hexagon
Perimeter = _____ cm	Perimeter = _____ in.
Trapezoid	Rhombus
Perimeter = _____ in.	Perimeter = _____ cm

♦ *Math Masters,* p. 499

Example 2: 3-Dimensional Geometry

Kindergarten and *First Grade Everyday Mathematics* have exposed children to geometric concepts. In *Second Grade Everyday Mathematics,* geometry Explorations have been part of previous units and have provided preliminary exposure to two- and three-dimensional geometric ideas.

Time Frame: Use Class Progress Indicator assessments with or after Lessons 5.7 and 9.7.

In Unit 5, children explore similarities and differences among three-dimensional shapes, such as prisms, pyramids, cylinders, cones, and spheres. They identify 2-D shapes, name points and line segments, and explore the notion of symmetry. We suggest that you conduct the initial assessment for geometry as part of Lesson 5.7, using *Math Journal 1,* page 127. This page provides a good indication of children's ability to classify various representations of 3-D shapes.

Sample 3-Dimensional Geometry Rubric

Sample Rubric
Beginning (B) Children use nongeometric names (for example, *ball* instead of *sphere*), but have difficulty seeing how objects can be matched to geometric shapes.
Developing (D) Children can name many of the three-dimensional shapes, but have difficulty classifying less common shapes (for example, calling a triangular prism a pyramid). They have minor difficulties identifying objects with these names or finding examples of some geometric shapes.
Secure (S) Children can name and classify common three-dimensional shapes correctly and match these to objects in the room or in the world.

NOTE: Use the information from this assessment to help plan instruction. If you have a number of children who are classified as Beginning, plan to work with them individually or in a small group.

For Secure children, you may wish to challenge them to find and classify more difficult geometric shapes, such as hemispheres, truncated cones (some round garbage cans), ellipsoids (regular egg shapes), tori (plural for *torus:* doughnut shapes), helixes (wire bindings), or common three-dimensional shapes that partially fit or are combinations of such geometric shapes as cylindrical bottles, lightbulbs, vases, milk cartons, roof shapes, and so forth.

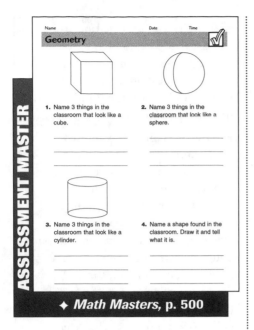

◆ Math Masters, p. 500

The second assessment could be done as part of Lesson 9.7, using *Math Masters,* page 500. (You may wish to use this page twice, once sometime after completing Unit 7 and again following Lesson 9.7.)

Alternative **progress-based assessment** can be done during the Explorations lesson, Lesson 9.7. While the rest of the class works at the Exploration stations, seat yourself at one station with a group of students. Have them sort objects that you brought in (baseball, box, soft-drink can, funnel) into geometric categories (sphere, rectangular prism, cylinder, and cone), much as you did with the Shapes Museum.

Class Checklists and Individual Profiles of Progress

Class Checklists and Individual Profiles of Progress are provided for each unit as well as for each quarter. These checklist and profile masters list the learning goals identified for the end-of-unit oral and written assessments. They are found at the back of your *Math Masters* book and are in the Assessment Master section of this book on pages 96–114.

First, use the Class Checklists to gather and record information. Then, transfer selected information to the Individual Profiles of Progress sheet for each child's portfolio or for use during parent conferences.

The information recorded on the checklists can be obtained from end-of-unit oral and written assessments. In fact, you may want to bypass the Class Checklists and record this information from these assessments directly onto the Individual Profiles of Progress.

Blank profile and checklist masters can be found in *Math Masters,* pages 485 and 486. You may wish to record information from other sources, such as journal review pages, Math Boxes, Math Messages, and Math Logs.

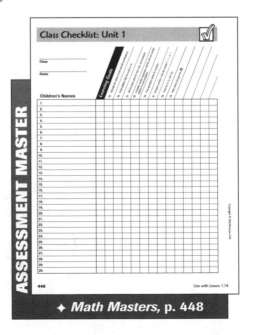

◆ Math Masters, p. 448

Information obtained from teacher-directed small groups, organized during Explorations, game time, or any other time is also a good resource to be recorded on the Class Checklists or directly on Individual Profiles of Progress. As mentioned in the Ongoing Assessment section of this book, information can be obtained from observations, questions, and other sources during regular instructional interactions as well.

When you use Class Checklists and Individual Profiles of Progress, consider using a rubric-recording method, such as Beginning, Developing, or Secure, to indicate progress. After children have had more experience and time with various concepts and skills, repeat needed assessment activities to assess progress further.

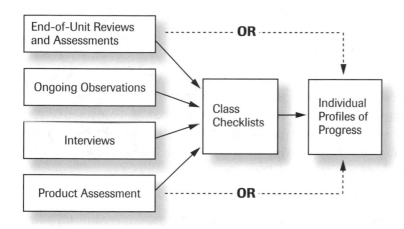

NOTE: Class Checklists and Individual Profiles of Progress are only two parts of your assessment program. Observations of children as they work, as well as samples of their work, are necessary to provide a full picture of children's understandings and abilities.

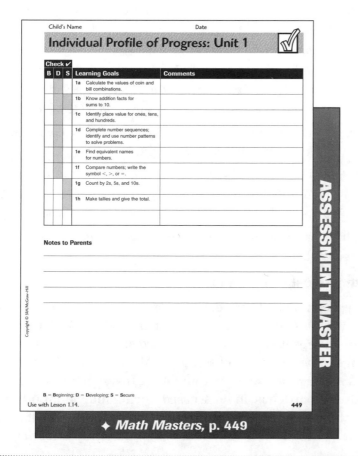

◆ *Math Masters*, p. 449

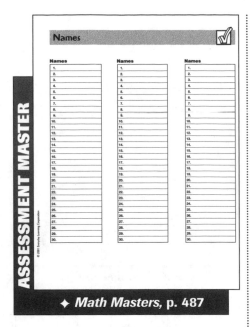

◆ Math Masters, p. 487

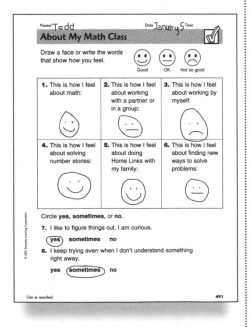

As an additional resource, you may choose to use *Math Masters,* page 487, which provides additional blank "Names" columns if you need to change the order for listing children's names on your master Class Checklist.

Individual Mathematical Interviews

Periodically interview children individually over the course of the year. These interviews should be kept short (10 to 15 minutes long, at most). Getting to each child is not something that can be done very often, but even a couple of times a year should suffice.

Main objectives of interviews
• To show children that you are concerned about them as individuals
• To get to know children better
• To find out how children feel about mathematics and what they know about it

When to hold interviews

Interviews can be conducted while the rest of the class is playing games or during fairly independent Explorations. Teachers have also suggested that, if feasible, you can make "appointments" to have lunch with children individually or with two or three children at a time. Other appointments might be arranged before class begins, during recess, or after school.

Suggestions for starting interviews

The focus of these interviews should reflect the information you are interested in discovering from individual children. Sample questions you may want to ask are:

• *How do you feel about mathematics?*

• *What have you enjoyed most about mathematics this year? What has been the easiest part of mathematics for you?*

• *What has been the hardest part of mathematics for you?*

• *How can we work together to help you feel more comfortable with these difficult parts of mathematics?*

• *How do you feel about working with partners and in small groups for some mathematics activities?*

• *How do you feel about Home Links? About Math Boxes?*

Children's responses might be taped or recorded on an individual interview sheet.

Math Interest Inventories

At the beginning of the year, you may want children to complete an inventory to assess their mathematical attitudes. This inventory might be repeated later in the year to see if their attitudes have changed. Two grade-level samples (About My Math Class) are given in *Math Masters,* pages 491 and 492. Inventories can be included in children's portfolios and discussed during individual interviews or parent conferences. For younger children, discussion of portfolios might be best done in individual or small-group interviews.

Parent Reflections

Parents can also be included in the assessment process. Prior to conferences, you can send parents a Parent Reflections page. A sample is given below. A blank Parent Reflections form is provided in *Math Masters,* page 489. The prompts are designed to focus parents' concerns prior to conferences.

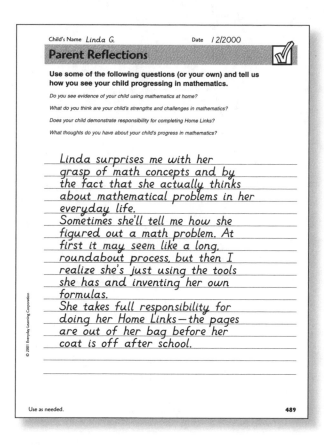

Your Assessment Ideas

_____

_____

_____

_____

_____

_____

_____

_____

_____

_____

_____

_____

_____

_____

_____

_____

_____

_____

_____

_____

_____

_____

_____

_____

_____

_____

Outside Tests

Many teachers are responsible for outside tests or assessments that are mandated by their schools, districts, or states. These tests vary widely, from traditional standardized tests with multiple-choice responses to more performance-based assessments. Because of the attention that is sometimes given to outside tests and assessments, many teachers worry whether *Everyday Mathematics* adequately prepares students, especially for the traditional standardized test formats.

Reports from teachers and school administrators indicate that *Everyday Mathematics* children generally do about as well on the computation sections of standardized tests—and much better on the concepts and problem-solving sections as students in traditional programs. Our research supports these anecdotal reports. However, traditional standardized tests do not assess the depth and breadth of the mathematical knowledge that should be attained in a well-implemented *Everyday Mathematics* classroom.

Many testing companies, as well as several states, districts, and schools, have recently developed performance assessments or open-ended tests. These tests indicate results similar to those from traditional tests—class and individual norms (percentile rankings)—but they also attempt to test problem-solving and communication skills on larger tasks. Some of these assessments provide rubric scores along with normed data.

Some standardized tests, along with many state tests, now allow the use of calculators on problem-solving sections because many students have access to them during instruction. Here are some further suggestions for handling outside tests:

- Rather than taking class time to "teach to the test," you may want to rely on Math Boxes and a systematic review of completed Math Boxes problems to help prepare children for the format of an outside test. It is our experience that it is the unfamiliar format and the test-taking conditions that disturb children, especially younger children, the most when taking outside tests.

NOTE: There are blank Math Boxes masters in the Teaching Aid Masters section of your *Math Masters* book (pages 218 and 219). You might want to use these to fill in your own Math Boxes problems.

- If your district test is based on traditional goals, work toward having it rewritten to match the National Council of Teachers of Mathematics *Assessment Standards* and the *Everyday Mathematics* curriculum.
- Encourage or consider the use of one of the newer performance-based tests in place of the traditional multiple-choice standardized tests. As much as possible, outside tests should reflect the instructional practices of the classroom.

Your Assessment Ideas

_____

_____

_____

_____

_____

_____

_____

_____

_____

_____

_____

_____

_____

_____

_____

_____

_____

_____

_____

_____

_____

_____

_____

Recommended Reading

Black, Paul, and Dylan Wiliam. "Assessment and Classroom Learning." *Assessment in Education* (March, 1998): 7–74.

———. "Inside the Black Box: Raising Standards Through Classroom Assessment." *Phi Delta Kappan* 80, no. 2 (October, 1998): 139–149.

Bryant, Brian R., and Teddy Maddox. "Using Alternative Assessment Techniques to Plan and Evaluate Mathematics." *LD Forum* 21, no. 2 (winter, 1996): 24–33.

Eisner, Elliot W. "The Uses and Limits of Performance Assessment." *Phi Delta Kappan* 80, no. 9 (May, 1999): 658–661.

Kuhn, Gerald. *Mathematics Assessment: What Works in the Classroom.* San Francisco: Jossey-Bass Publishers, 1994.

National Council of Teachers of Mathematics (NCTM). *Curriculum and Evaluation Standards for School Mathematics.* Reston, Va.: NCTM, 1989.

———. *Assessment Standards for School Mathematics.* Reston, Va.: NCTM, 1995.

———. *Principles and Standards for School Mathematics: Discussion Draft.* Prepared by the Standards 2000 Writing Group. Reston, Va.: NCTM, 1998.

National Research Council, Mathematical Sciences Education Board. *Measuring What Counts: A Conceptual Guide for Mathematics Assessment.* Washington, D.C.: National Academy Press, 1993.

Pearson, Bethyl, and Cathy Berghoff. "London Bridge Is Not Falling Down: It's Supporting Alternative Assessment." *TESOL* Journal 5, no. 4 (summer, 1996): 28–31.

Shepard, Lorrie A. "Using Assessment to Improve Learning." *Educational Leadership* 52, no. 5 (February, 1995): 38–43.

Stenmark, Jean Kerr, ed. *Mathematics Assessment: Myths, Models, Good Questions, and Practical Suggestions.* Reston, Va.: National Council of Teachers of Mathematics, 1991.

Stiggens, Richard J. *Student-Centered Classroom Assessment.* Englewood Cliffs, N.J.: Prentice-Hall, 1997.

Webb, N. L., and A. F. Coxford, eds. *Assessment in the Mathematics Classroom: 1993 Yearbook.* Reston, Va.: National Council of Teachers of Mathematics, 1993.

Your Assessment Ideas

Assessment Overviews

This section offers examples for each unit of how to use different types of assessments in specific lessons. For each unit, you will find examples of three major types of assessment opportunities: Ongoing Assessment, Product Assessment, and Periodic Assessment. Keep in mind, however, that these are not distinct categories; they frequently overlap. For example, some Periodic Assessments may also serve as Product Assessments that you or the child may choose to keep in the child's portfolio.

Unit 1
Assessment Overview

There are many pathways to a balanced assessment plan. As you teach Unit 1, start to become familiar with some of the approaches to assessment. The next few pages provide examples of the three major types of assessment suggested in this program: Ongoing Assessment, Product Assessment, and Periodic Assessment. This assessment overview offers examples of ways to assess children on what they learn in Unit 1. Do not try to use all of the examples, but begin with a few that meet your needs.

Ongoing Assessment Opportunities

Ongoing assessment opportunities are opportunities to observe children during regular interactions, as they work independently and in groups. You can conduct ongoing assessment during teacher-guided instruction, Math Boxes sessions, mathematical mini-interviews, games, Mental Math and Reflexes sessions, strategy sharing, and slate work. The chart below provides a summary of ongoing assessment opportunities in Unit 1, as they relate to specific Unit 1 learning goals.

1a	**Developing Goal** Calculate the values of coin and bill combinations. (Lessons 1.2, 1.6, and 1.12)	Lesson 1.6, p. 42 Lesson 1.12, p. 67
1b	**Developing/Secure Goal** Know addition facts for sums to 10. (Lessons 1.2 and 1.4)	Lesson 1.4, p. 33
1d	**Developing Goal** Complete number sequences; identify and use number patterns to solve problems. (Lessons 1.1 and 1.8)	Lesson 1.1, p. 17
1e	**Developing Goal** Find equivalent names for numbers. (Lessons 1.10 and 1.11)	Lesson 1.10, p. 59
1f	**Developing Goal** Compare numbers; write the symbol $<$, $>$, or $=$. (Lesson 1.12)	Lesson 1.12, p. 67

Product Assessment Opportunities

Math Journals, Math Boxes, activity sheets, masters, Math Logs, and the results of Explorations and Projects all provide product assessment opportunities. On the next page is an example of how you might use a rubric to assess children's ability to make number scrolls.

ENRICHMENT Making Individual Number Scrolls

Children make individual scrolls, beginning with a number with which they are comfortable. Use multiple copies of *Math Masters*, page 14 for making scrolls.

Sample Rubric
Beginning (B)
The child begins the number scroll incorrectly or needs assistance from the teacher to get started. For example, the number 100 may appear as the first number on the top line to the far left of the scroll. As the child fills in the scroll, some numbers may be omitted, resulting in a scroll that does not have uniform patterns going down a column or across a row.
Developing (D)
The child begins the number scroll correctly and without teacher assistance. Typically, he or she will begin with a larger number, such as 501. The child may encounter some difficulties in writing the numbers. As a result, the pattern may appear incorrect. The child may still have difficulty going from, for example, 699 to 700.
Secure (S)
The child begins the number scroll correctly and without teacher assistance. The child may begin with such a number as 1,001 or higher. He or she has little or no difficulty writing the numbers in the correct sequence, resulting in the appropriate patterns. The child may continue to scroll well into the thousands.

Periodic Assessment Opportunities

Here is a summary of the periodic assessment opportunities that are provided in Unit 1. Refer to Lesson 1.14 for details.

Oral and Slate Assessment

In Lesson 1.14, you will find oral and slate assessment problems on pages 76–78.

Written Assessment

In Lesson 1.14, you will find written assessment problems on page 78 (*Math Masters*, page 419).

See the chart on the next page to find oral, slate, and written assessment problems that address specific learning goals.

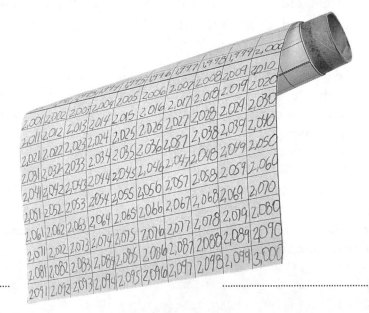

1a **Developing Goal** Calculate the values of coin and bill combinations. (Lessons 1.2, 1.6, and 1.12)	Oral Assessment, Problem 5 Slate Assessment, Problem 11 Written Assessment, Problems 2 and 6
1b **Developing/Secure Goal** Know addition facts for sums to 10. (Lessons 1.2 and 1.4)	Slate Assessment, Problems 2, 8, and 9 Written Assessment, Problem 4
1c **Developing Goal** Identify place value for ones, tens, and hundreds. (Lesson 1.9)	Slate Assessment, Problems 4–6 Written Assessment, Problem 3
1d **Developing Goal** Complete number sequences; identify and use number patterns to solve problems. (Lessons 1.1 and 1.8)	Slate Assessment, Problem 1 Written Assessment, Problem 5
1e **Developing Goal** Find equivalent names for numbers. (Lessons 1.10 and 1.11)	Slate Assessment, Problem 3 Written Assessment, Problem 7
1f **Developing Goal** Compare numbers; write the symbol $<$, $>$, or $=$. (Lesson 1.12)	Slate Assessment, Problem 7
1g **Secure Goal** Count by 2s, 5s, and 10s. (Lesson 1.11)	Oral Assessment, Problems 1–4
1h **Secure Goal** Make tallies and give the total. (Lesson 1.5)	Written Assessment, Problem 1

Alternative Assessment

In Lesson 1.14, you will find alternative assessment options on page 78.

✦ **Play *Digit Discovery***

As children play this game from Lesson 1.12, assess their understanding of place value. Use a Class Checklist or Flip Cards to record children's understanding of ones, tens, and hundreds. Encourage children to write the new number on a sheet of paper. Use these papers to assess children's ability to write numbers.

• Did the child understand such terms as 500 less, 10 less, 10 more, the smallest 3-digit number, and so forth?

• Did the child have difficulty knowing when to change a number?

• Did the child know when to utilize his or her number?

✦ **Create Number-Grid Puzzles**

Use this activity to assess children's understanding of the number grid. Children create number-grid puzzle pieces and then arrange them on a blank number grid. In doing so, they will need to identify and use number-grid patterns. Use a Class Checklist or Flip Cards to record children's understanding of number patterns. Consider such questions as the following as you assess children's progress:

• Did the child identify and use various number-grid patterns (such as 1 more, 10 more, 1 less, and 10 less)?

• Were the puzzle grid pieces placed in the appropriate locations on the blank number grid?

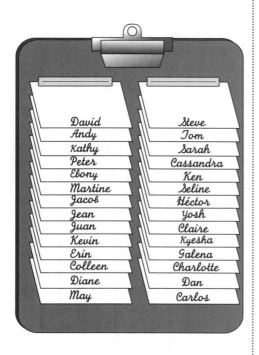

David · Steve
Andy · Tom
Kathy · Sarah
Peter · Cassandra
Ebony · Ken
Martine · Seline
Jacob · Héctor
Jean · Yosh
Juan · Claire
Kevin · Kyesha
Erin · Galena
Colleen · Charlotte
Diane · Dan
May · Carlos

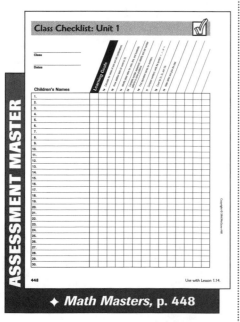

ASSESSMENT MASTER

Class Checklist: Unit 1

Class
Dates

Children's Names

448   Use with Lesson 1.14.

✦ *Math Masters*, p. 448

Unit 2
Assessment Overview

If you tried some of the assessment approaches that were suggested in the Unit 1 Assessment Overview, you are probably beginning to appreciate how the goal charts can help you plan your assessment strategies. For example, at this point children are expected to be at a Secure level for the "easier" addition facts (see Goal 2f in the chart below), and the chart alerts you to the fact that ongoing assessment opportunities related to that goal are provided in four different lessons. In a similar fashion, you can use the chart on page 45 to find slate and written assessment opportunities related to this same goal.

Ongoing Assessment Opportunities

Ongoing assessment opportunities are opportunities to observe children during regular interactions, as they work independently and in groups. You can conduct ongoing assessment during teacher-guided instruction, Math Boxes sessions, mathematical mini-interviews, games, Mental Math and Reflexes sessions, strategy sharing, and slate work. The chart below provides a summary of ongoing assessment opportunities in Unit 2, as they relate to specific Unit 2 learning goals.

2b	**Developing/Secure Goal** Know "harder" addition facts. (Lessons 2.4 and 2.5)	Lesson 2.5, p. 111
2c	**Developing/Secure Goal** Know "easier" subtraction facts. (Lessons 2.8 and 2.12)	Lesson 2.9, p. 131 Lesson 2.10, p. 136
2e	**Developing/Secure Goal** Solve subtraction number stories. (Lessons 2.6 and 2.9)	Lesson 2.9, p. 131
2f	**Secure Goal** Know "easier" addition facts. (Lessons 2.2, 2.3, 2.5, and 2.8–2.10)	Lesson 2.3, p. 103 Lesson 2.5, p. 111 Lesson 2.9, p. 131 Lesson 2.10, p. 136
2g	**Developing/Secure Goal** Construct fact families for addition and subtraction. (Lessons 2.6 and 2.8)	Lesson 2.6, p. 116
2j	**Secure Goal** Find equivalent names for numbers. (Lessons 2.9 and 2.10)	Lesson 2.9, p. 131 Lesson 2.10, p. 136

Product Assessment Opportunities

Math Journals, Math Boxes, activity sheets, masters, Math Logs, and the results of Explorations and Projects all provide product assessment opportunities. Here is an example of how you might use a rubric to assess children's ability to solve addition and subtraction number stories.

Lesson 2.14, p. 155

ALTERNATIVE ASSESSMENT **Write and Solve Addition and Subtraction Number Stories**

Use *Math Masters,* page 22 to assess children's understanding of writing and solving number stories. As children write their stories, you will see who understands the operations, number models, mental arithmetic, and mathematical language involved. The sample rubric below can help you evaluate children's work.

Portfolio Ideas

Sample Rubric
Beginning (B) The child needs assistance in getting started. The number story is incomplete—data may not be given, units may not be assigned to the data in the problem, a question may not be posed, or the question that is posed cannot be answered from the information given. The child does not include most of the components needed for a number story.
Developing (D) The child attempts to write and solve the number story without assistance. The child writes a number story, and it contains most of the number-story components.
Secure (S) The child writes a number story without assistance that contains all or most of the following components: unit, picture, number model, and question. The story is answered correctly.

Periodic Assessment Opportunities

Here is a summary of the periodic assessment opportunities that are provided in Unit 2. Refer to Lesson 2.14 for details.

Oral and Slate Assessment

In Lesson 2.14, you will find oral and slate assessment problems on pages 153 and 154.

Written Assessment

In Lesson 2.14, you will find written assessment problems on page 154 (*Math Masters,* pages 420 and 421).

See the chart on the next page to find slate and written assessment problems that address specific learning goals.

2a	**Developing Goal** Know "harder" subtraction facts. (Lesson 2.13)	Slate Assessment, Problems 10 and 11 Written Assessment, Problem 8
2b	**Developing/Secure Goal** Know "harder" addition facts. (Lessons 2.4 and 2.5)	Slate Assessment, Problem 7 Written Assessment, Problem 6
2c	**Developing/Secure Goal** Know "easier" subtraction facts. (Lessons 2.8 and 2.12)	Slate Assessment, Problem 9 Written Assessment, Problem 7
2d	**Developing/Secure Goal** Complete "What's My Rule?" tables. (Lesson 2.11)	Written Assessment, Problem 4
2e	**Developing/Secure Goal** Solve subtraction number stories. (Lessons 2.6 and 2.9)	Slate Assessment, Problems 9, 10, and 11
2f	**Secure Goal** Know "easier" addition facts. (Lessons 2.2, 2.3, 2.5, and 2.8–2.10)	Slate Assessment, Problems 6 and 8 Written Assessment, Problem 5
2g	**Developing/Secure Goal** Construct fact families for addition and subtraction. (Lessons 2.6 and 2.8)	Slate Assessment, Problem 2 Written Assessment, Problem 1
2h	**Developing/Secure Goal** Complete Frames-and-Arrows diagrams. (Lesson 2.10)	Written Assessment, Problem 3
2i	**Secure Goal** Solve addition stories. (Lesson 2.1)	Slate Assessment, Problems 6, 7, and 8
2j	**Secure Goal** Find equivalent names for numbers. (Lessons 2.9 and 2.10)	Slate Assessment, Problem 3 Written Assessment, Problem 2

Alternative Assessment

In Lesson 2.14, you will find alternative assessment options on page 155.

✦ Use +, − Fact Triangles

As pairs of children use the Fact Triangles, assess children's knowledge of addition and subtraction facts and fact families. As you circulate, use a Class Checklist or Flip Cards to record children's progress. You also could have children record on a half-sheet of paper the facts they still need to practice.

• Did the child utilize the fact strategies taught?

• Did the child see the relationships among the facts in the fact families?

• If a child knew an addition fact, was he or she able to give the answer to a subtraction fact within the fact family?

• Does the child have fact automaticity?

✦ Write and Solve Addition and Subtraction Number Stories

Use this activity to assess children's understanding of operations, number models, mental arithmetic, and mathematical language. Children write their number stories on *Math Masters,* page 22. To help assess children's understanding, a sample rubric is provided on page 44 in the Product Assessment section of this handbook.

Portfolio Ideas

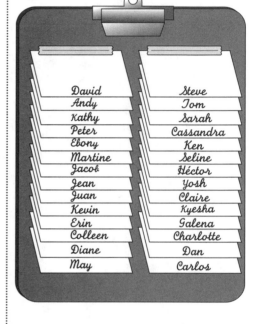

✦ *Math Masters,* p. 450

ASSESSMENT MASTER

Unit 3
Assessment Overview

The focus of this unit is on place value, money, and time. At this stage in their learning, children should be at a Secure level for showing all penny, nickel, dime, and quarter combinations for a given amount of money (see Goal 3f in the chart below), and the chart indicates that an ongoing assessment opportunity related to this goal can be found in Lesson 3.2 on page 175 of the *Teacher's Lesson Guide*. Similarly, the chart on page 48 indicates where you can find a written assessment problem to help you assess children's progress toward this same goal.

Ongoing Assessment Opportunities

Ongoing assessment opportunities are opportunities to observe children during regular interactions, as they work independently and in groups. You can conduct ongoing assessment during teacher-guided instruction, Math Boxes sessions, mathematical mini-interviews, games, Mental Math and Reflexes sessions, strategy sharing, and slate work. The chart below provides a summary of ongoing assessment opportunities in Unit 3, as they relate to specific Unit 3 learning goals.

3a	**Developing Goal** Solve Frames-and-Arrows problems having two rules. (Lessons 3.3 and 3.6)	Lesson 3.3, p. 181
3b	**Developing Goal** Make change. (Lessons 3.2, 3.7, and 3.8)	Lesson 3.7, p. 199 Lesson 3.8, p. 205
3c	**Developing Goal** Know "harder" subtraction facts. (Lesson 3.5)	Lesson 3.5, p. 192
3f	**Secure Goal** Show ⓅⓃⒹ and Ⓠ for a given amount. (Lesson 3.2)	Lesson 3.2, p. 175
3g	**Secure Goal** Know addition facts. (Lesson 3.5)	Lesson 3.5, p. 192
3h	**Secure Goal** Know "easier" subtraction facts. (Lesson 3.5)	Lesson 3.5, p. 192

Product Assessment Opportunities

Math Journals, Math Boxes, activity sheets, masters, Math Logs, and the results of Explorations and Projects all provide product assessment opportunities. Here are some ideas for assessing children's work products in Unit 3.

Lesson 3.6, p. 197

ENRICHMENT **Making Up and Solving Frames-and-Arrows Problems Having Two Rules**

Children use *Math Masters,* page 56 to create and then solve Frames-and-Arrows problems that have two rules. The sample rubric below can help you evaluate children's work.

Sample Rubric

Beginning (B)
The child attempts to start the activity but requires much teacher assistance throughout most of it. The child has difficulty using two different rules. Perhaps the child uses only one rule instead of two or uses small numbers. The child also has difficulty solving similar problems and, once again, requires teacher assistance.

Developing (D)
The child attempts to create a Frames-and-Arrows problem with two rules. Little assistance is needed, except when using larger numbers. A few errors are made, or the correct rule is not given. The child may be able to complete a set of two-rule problems with some assistance.

Secure (S)
The child creates Frames-and-Arrows problems that have two rules without teacher assistance. The child uses both addition and subtraction that involve 2-digit and 3-digit numbers. He or she is able to create Frames-and-Arrows problems that require the child to produce the rule, or problems in which the first frame is not filled in. The child is also able to solve a set of two-rule problems independently.

Periodic Assessment Opportunities

Here is a summary of the periodic assessment opportunities that are provided in Unit 3. Refer to Lesson 3.9 for details.

Oral and Slate Assessment

In Lesson 3.9, you will find oral and slate assessment problems on pages 208 and 209.

Written Assessment

In Lesson 3.9, you will find written assessment problems on page 210 (*Math Masters,* pages 422 and 423).

See the chart on the next page to find oral, slate, and written assessment problems that address specific learning goals.

3a	**Developing Goal** Solve Frames-and-Arrows problems having two rules. (Lessons 3.3 and 3.6)	Written Assessment, Problems 2 and 3
3b	**Developing Goal** Make change. (Lessons 3.2, 3.7, and 3.8)	Written Assessment, Problems 4 and 5
3c	**Developing Goal** Know "harder" subtraction facts. (Lesson 3.5)	Slate Assessment, Problem 9
3d	**Developing/Secure Goal** Tell time to 5-minute intervals. (Lessons 3.3 and 3.4)	Slate Assessment, Problem 4 Written Assessment, Problems 6–9
3e	**Developing/Secure Goal** Identify place value in 2-digit and 3-digit numbers. (Lessons 3.1 and 3.4)	Oral Assessment Slate Assessment, Problems 1–3
3f	**Secure Goal** Show Ⓟ,Ⓝ,Ⓓ, and Ⓠ for a given amount. (Lesson 3.2)	Written Assessment, Problem 1
3g	**Secure Goal** Know addition facts. (Lesson 3.5)	Slate Assessment, Problem 7
3h	**Secure Goal** Know "easier" subtraction facts. (Lesson 3.5)	Slate Assessment, Problem 8

Alternative Assessment

In Lesson 3.9, you will find alternative assessment options on pages 210 and 211.

✦ Use Addition/Subtraction Fact Triangles

As children practice their addition and subtraction facts independently or in pairs, use the Class Checklist or Flip Cards to record children's fact-power abilities. Children should focus on the "harder" addition/subtraction facts. You may also consider having them record the facts that they still need to practice on a half-sheet of paper. As you assess children's abilities, keep the following questions in mind:

• Does the child have fact automaticity for the "easy" addition/subtraction facts?

• Did the child utilize fact strategies (doubles, plus 9, and so forth) when needed?

✦ Play *Making Change*

As children play this game from Lesson 3.8 (*Math Journal 1,* page 78), assess their ability to make change. Record observations on a Class Checklist or on Flip Cards. You may also consider asking children to record their transactions on a sheet of paper divided into three columns labeled *Amount of Money I Owe the Bank, Amount of Money I Put into the Bank,* and *My Change.* Keep such questions as the following in mind as you assess children's ability to make change:

• Was the child able to give the bank a correct amount of money?

• Was the child able to make change if necessary?

✦ Use Clock Booklets

Use the clock booklets that children made in Lesson 3.4 (*Math Masters,* pages 45 and 46), to assess their time-telling skills. Place stick-on notes on the digital notation or on the clock face in children's clock booklets. Then ask children either to record the time in digital notation on a half-sheet of paper or to draw the time on a clock face. Collect the half-sheets of paper and booklets to assess progress, keeping the following questions in mind:

• Was the child able to identify and write the correct digital time when looking at a clock?

• Was the child able to draw the correct time on a clock face when given the digital time?

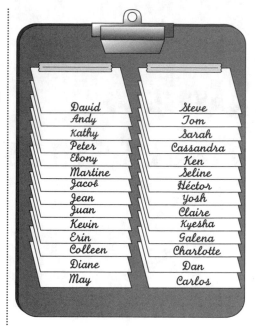

✦ *Math Masters,* p. 452

Unit 4
Assessment Overview

At this point in the *Everyday Mathematics* program, you may consider whether you are beginning to establish a balance of Ongoing, Product, and Periodic Assessment strategies. Also, think about whether your strategies include both keeping anecdotal records based on observations of children's progress and using written assessments. Don't be afraid to try some different assessment strategies. Make note of those strategies that work best for you.

Ongoing Assessment Opportunities

Ongoing assessment opportunities are opportunities to observe children during regular interactions, as they work independently and in groups. You can conduct ongoing assessment during teacher-guided instruction, Math Boxes sessions, mathematical mini-interviews, games, Mental Math and Reflexes sessions, strategy sharing, and slate work. The chart below provides a summary of ongoing assessment opportunities in Unit 4, as they relate to specific Unit 4 learning goals.

4a	**Developing Goal** Devise and use strategies for finding sums of 2-digit numbers. (Lessons 4.1 and 4.6–4.9)	Lesson 4.1, p. 227 Lesson 4.9, p. 273
4d	**Developing Goal** Read °F on a thermometer. (Lessons 4.3 and 4.4)	Lesson 4.3, p. 237
4e	**Developing/Secure Goal** Add and subtract with multiples of 10. (Lessons 4.1–4.3 and 4.6–4.9)	Lesson 4.6, p. 254

Product Assessment Opportunities

Math Journals, Math Boxes, activity sheets, masters, Math Logs, and the results of Explorations and Projects all provide product assessment opportunities. On the next page is an example of how you might use a rubric to assess children's ability to use pattern-block designs.

Lesson 4.9, p. 274

ENRICHMENT **Exploring Pattern-Block Designs**

Children use a variety of pattern-block shapes to cover hexagons on *Math Masters*, pages 72 and 73. They record their work by using the template and by making colored Xs to match the actual colors of the pattern blocks. The sample rubric below can help you evaluate children's understanding.

Portfolio Ideas

Sample Rubric
Beginning (B)
The child has difficulty getting started and needs some teacher assistance. Most of the hexagons are covered with only one pattern-block shape. The child also has difficulty transferring the pattern-block shapes using the template.
Developing (D)
The child is able to complete most, but not all, of the activity without teacher assistance. Some of the hexagons are covered with a variety of pattern-block shapes. Using the template, the child may be able to transfer the pattern-block shapes using the template.
Secure (S)
With little or no assistance, the child is able to cover all of the hexagons using at least two different kinds of pattern-block shapes. He or she might also look for more solutions than required. Using the template, the child is also able to transfer his or her work from the pattern-block shapes.

Periodic Assessment Opportunities

Here is a summary of the periodic assessment opportunities that are provided in Unit 4. Refer to Lesson 4.10 for details.

Oral and Slate Assessment

In Lesson 4.10, you will find slate assessment problems on pages 276 and 277.

Written Assessment

In Lesson 4.10, you will find written assessment problems on page 278 (*Math Masters*, pages 424 and 425).

See the chart below to find slate and written assessment problems that address specific learning goals.

4a **Developing Goal** Devise and use strategies for finding sums of 2-digit numbers. (Lessons 4.1 and 4.6–4.9)	Slate Assessment, Problem 1 Written Assessment, Problems 1, 2, and 9–12
4b **Developing Goal** Devise and use strategies for finding differences of 2-digit numbers. (Lesson 4.4)	Slate Assessment, Problem 2 Written Assessment, Problems 3 and 4
4c **Developing Goal** Estimate approximate costs and sums. (Lessons 4.5 and 4.8)	Slate Assessment, Problems 3 and 4
4d **Developing Goal** Read °F on a thermometer. (Lessons 4.3 and 4.4)	Written Assessment, Problems 5–8
4e **Developing/Secure Goal** Add and subtract with multiples of 10. (Lessons 4.1–4.3 and 4.6–4.9)	Slate Assessment, Problems 1 and 2

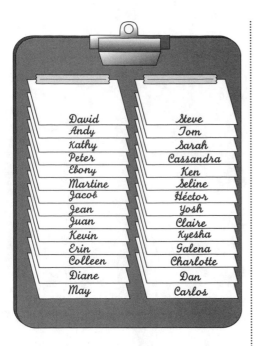

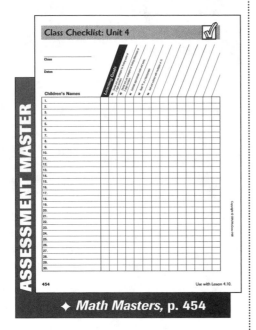

♦ Math Masters, p. 454

Alternative Assessment

In Lesson 4.10, you will find alternative assessment options on pages 278 and 279.

✦ **Play *Shopping***

As children play *Shopping* from Lesson 4.6 (*Math Journal 1*, page 97), assess their ability to add 2-digit numbers. Use a Class Checklist or Flip Cards to record children's understanding. Ask them to record their number models on sheets of paper. Each number model should include *part, part,* and *total*. Some children may still need to draw the actual diagram in order to solve the problem. Collect the sheets when students are finished, and think about such questions as the following:

• Was the child able to generate a number model from the two shopping cards selected?

• Did the child give a correct total?

• Did the child rely on using the money to generate the total?

✦ **Play *Addition Spin***

Assess children's ability to add 2-digit numbers by having them play *Addition Spin* from Lesson 4.2 (*Math Journal 1*, page 86). Select a spin mat from *Math Masters,* pages 61 or 62, depending on the skill level you want to assess. You may customize the spin mat for children who are ready to move on to addition with regrouping. Ask children to record their work on a sheet of paper.

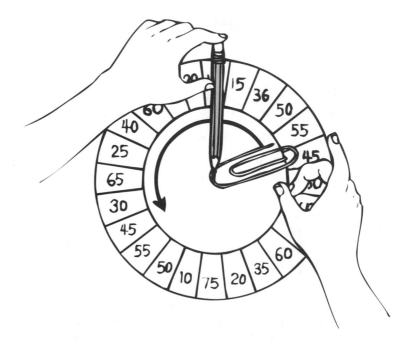

Unit 5
Assessment Overview

A major topic of this unit is understanding 2-dimensional shapes. Children are expected to be at a Secure level for identifying 2-dimensional shapes (see Goal 5f in the chart segment below). This chart segment indicates where you can find an ongoing assessment opportunity related to this goal. In addition, the chart on page 54 indicates where you can find written problems to help you assess children's progress toward this same goal.

Ongoing Assessment Opportunities

Ongoing assessment opportunities are opportunities to observe children during regular interactions, as they work independently and in groups. You can conduct ongoing assessment during teacher-guided instruction, Math Boxes sessions, mathematical mini-interviews, games, Mental Math and Reflexes sessions, strategy sharing, and slate work. The chart segment below suggests an ongoing assessment opportunity in Unit 5, as it relates to a specific Unit 5 learning goal.

Secure Goal Identify 2-dimensional shapes. (Lessons 5.2, 5.3, and 5.6)	Written Assessment, Problems 4 and 5

Product Assessment Opportunities

Math Journals, Math Boxes, activity sheets, masters, Math Logs, and the results of Explorations and Projects all provide product assessment opportunities. On the next page is an example of how you might use a rubric to assess children's understanding of equal sharing.

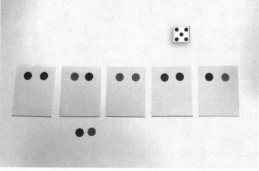

Lesson 5.2, p. 298

EXPLORATION F **Exploring Equal Sharing**

In this activity, the children's task is to share "eggs" equally among the "nests." Children record what they did, showing the number of eggs they started with, the number of nests, the number of eggs in each nest, and the number of eggs left over. The sample rubric below can help you evaluate children's work.

Portfolio Ideas

Sample Rubric
Beginning (B) The child is able to choose the number of "nests" and use the die to determine the number of "eggs" but has difficulty dividing the eggs equally among the nests. The child may place too many eggs in each nest initially so some nests do not have any eggs.
Developing (D) With some help, the child is able to divide the eggs equally among the nests but seems confused if the number does not come out even (if there is a remainder). Even in cases in which there are at least twice as many eggs as nests, the child is hesitant to place more than one egg in a nest at a time.
Secure (S) The child has no difficulty dividing the eggs equally among the nests, even when there are remainders. Little or no help is needed.

Periodic Assessment Opportunities

Here is a summary of the periodic assessment opportunities that are provided for Unit 5. Refer to Lesson 5.10 for details.

Oral and Slate Assessment

In Lesson 5.10, you will find slate assessment problems on pages 338 and 339.

Written Assessment

In Lesson 5.10, you will find written assessment problems on page 339 (*Math Masters,* pages 426 and 427).

See the chart below to find written assessment problems that address specific learning goals.

5a	**Developing Goal** Identify 3-dimensional shapes, such as rectangular prisms, cylinders, pyramids, cones, and spheres. (Lessons 5.7 and 5.8)	Written Assessment, Problems 6–8
5b	**Developing Goal** Identify symmetrical figures. (Lesson 5.9)	Written Assessment, Problem 9
5c	**Developing Goal** Find common attributes of shapes. (Lessons 5.1 and 5.2)	Written Assessment, Problem 10
5d	**Developing Goal** Identify parallel and nonparallel line segments. (Lesson 5.5)	Written Assessment, Problems 2 and 3
5e	**Secure Goal** Draw line segments. (Lessons 5.4 and 5.5)	Written Assessment, Problems 1–3
5f	**Secure Goal** Identify 2-dimensional shapes. (Lessons 5.2, 5.3, and 5.6)	Written Assessment, Problems 4 and 5

Alternative Assessment

In Lesson 5.10, you will find alternative assessment options on pages 340 and 341.

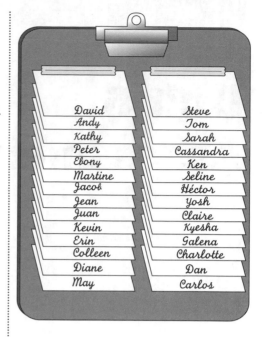

✦ Make Symmetrical Shapes

In Activity 1, children draw a design with pencil or crayon on a half-sheet of paper and then fold and rub the design onto the other half. Children then unfold the paper to reveal a symmetrical design. In Activity 2, they cut from a folded sheet of paper to make another symmetrical shape. After completing each activity, ask children such questions as:

• Was the design symmetrical? How did you know?

• Where was the line of symmetry?

✦ Use a Template to Draw a 6-Pointed Star

There are at least two different methods for drawing a 6-pointed star using geometrical shapes. As children discuss their methods, talk about their drawings. After volunteers have shared their methods with the class, you might provide help if children are unaware of the more common methods. Raise the following questions about the geometrical shapes used:

• Why is a 6-pointed star not a polygon?

• Why did you choose a hexagon (and triangle) to construct your star?

• How did the lengths of one side of the triangle and one side of the hexagon compare?

• Could you have used only hexagons to make the star? Only triangles?

✦ Color a Geometric Pattern

Children are asked to color a pattern using two or more colors. Then, they are asked to identify and trace with their fingers several different types of geometric figures. As you circulate, watch to see if children can correctly identify triangles, rhombuses, trapezoids, and hexagons. Raise such questions as the following:

• How were you able to tell which type of figure you were tracing?

• In what way was that (triangle, hexagon) different from a rhombus?

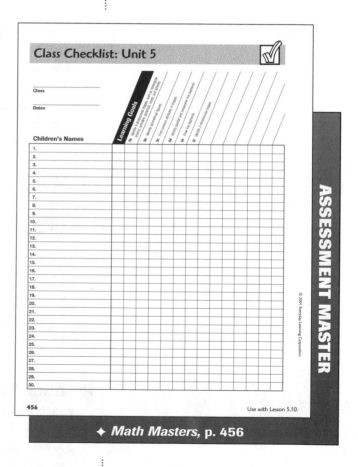

✦ *Math Masters*, p. 456

Unit 6
Assessment Overview

By the time they complete Unit 6, children should be Secure in their ability to add three 1-digit numbers mentally. To ensure this, you might consider providing children with a variety of regular review and practice opportunities related to this skill as you progress through the unit. As children begin some initial work with division, they also learn to think about these skills in terms of equal-sharing and equal-grouping stories.

Ongoing Assessment Opportunities

Ongoing assessment opportunities are opportunities to observe children during regular interactions, as they work independently and in groups. You can conduct ongoing assessment during teacher-guided instruction, Math Boxes sessions, mathematical mini-interviews, games, Mental Math and Reflexes sessions, strategy sharing, and slate work. The chart below provides a summary of ongoing assessment opportunities in Unit 6, as they relate to specific Unit 6 learning goals.

6c	**Developing Goal** Use the trade-first method to solve 2-digit subtraction problems. (Lessons 6.6, 6.10, and 6.12)	Lesson 6.6, p. 387
6f	**Developing Goal** Add three 2-digit numbers mentally. (Lessons 6.1, 6.2, 6.6, 6.7, and 6.11)	Lesson 6.1, p. 357 Lesson 6.2, p. 364 Lesson 6.7, p. 393
6h	**Developing/Secure Goal** Solve addition and subtraction number stories. (Lessons 6.2–6.4 and 6.7)	Lesson 6.4, p. 375
6i	**Secure Goal** Add three 1-digit numbers mentally. (Lessons 6.1, 6.2, 6.4, and 6.7)	Lesson 6.1, p. 357 Lesson 6.2, p. 364 Lesson 6.7, p. 393

Product Assessment Opportunities

Math Journals, Math Boxes, activity sheets, masters, Math Logs, and the results of Explorations and Projects all provide product assessment opportunities. On the next page is an example of how you might use a rubric to assess children's ability to make up and solve addition and subtraction number stories.

Lesson 6.4, p. 376

ENRICHMENT **Number Stories**

Circulate around the room as children work independently to write, illustrate, and find the solutions to number stories. The sample rubric below can help you evaluate children's work in this lesson, as well as in other number-story activities that appear later in this unit.

Portfolio Ideas

Sample Rubric
Beginning (B) The child attempts to write an addition and subtraction number story, but many of the components are missing. The child may attempt to solve the problem by using a diagram, but the diagram selected is incorrect. Teacher assistance is needed.
Developing (D) The child writes an addition and subtraction number story. Most of the components were included. Each of the stories is solved by drawing and using an appropriate diagram. The sum or difference might be incorrect because of a computational error. The number model may be missing.
Secure (S) The child writes an addition and subtraction number story containing all of the necessary components: an appropriate diagram to illustrate the story (a diagram that is filled in to represent known and unknown numbers), a correct sum or difference, and a number model to summarize the problem.

Periodic Assessment Opportunities

Here is a summary of the periodic assessment opportunities that are provided in Unit 6. Refer to Lesson 6.12 for details.

Oral and Slate Assessment

In Lesson 6.12, you will find oral and slate assessment problems on pages 417 and 418.

Written Assessment

In Lesson 6.12, you will find written assessment problems on page 419 (*Math Masters*, page 428).

See the chart below and on the next page to find oral, slate, and written assessment problems that address specific learning goals.

6a **Beginning/Developing Goal** Solve stories about multiples of equal groups. (Lessons 6.8, 6.9, and 6.11)	Oral Assessment, Problem 1
6b **Beginning/Developing Goal** Solve equal-grouping and equal-sharing division problems. (Lessons 6.11 and 6.12)	Oral Assessment, Problem 2
6c **Developing Goal** Use the trade-first method to solve 2-digit subtraction problems. (Lessons 6.6, 6.10, and 6.12)	Oral Assessment, Problems 2–4 Written Assessment, Problems 2–4
6d **Developing Goal** Make ballpark estimates of exact answers. (Lessons 6.1, 6.4, 6.6, 6.7, 6.10, and 6.11)	Slate Assessment, Problem 1

6e **Developing Goal** Model multiplication problems with arrays. (Lessons 6.9 and 6.10)	Oral Assessment, Problem 1 Written Assessment, Problems 5 and 6
6f **Developing Goal** Add three 2-digit numbers mentally. (Lessons 6.1, 6.2, 6.6, 6.7, and 6.11)	Written Assessment, Problem 1
6g **Developing/Secure Goal** Add and subtract with multiples of 10. (Lessons 6.1, 6.5, and 6.10)	Slate Assessment, Problem 2
6h **Developing/Secure Goal** Solve addition and subtraction number stories. (Lessons 6.2–6.4 and 6.7)	Slate Assessment, Problem 4 Written Assessment, Problems 7 and 8
6i **Secure Goal** Add three 1-digit numbers mentally. (Lessons 6.1, 6.2, 6.4, and 6.7)	Slate Assessment, Problem 3 Written Assessment, Problem 1

Alternative Assessment

In Lesson 6.12, you will find alternative assessment options on page 420.

✦ **Describe a Method to Solve a Multidigit Subtraction Problem**

Children solve two subtraction problems, one of which requires a trade and one of which does not. They must also describe the strategy that they used to solve each problem. Circulate and listen as children describe their strategies.

• Was each child able to use his or her method to correctly answer the problem?

• Did children display a clear understanding of place value?

✦ **Play *Three Addends***

As children play this game, circulate and assess whether they understand how to look for combinations of numbers that are easy to add.

• Was the child able to find which pair of numbers in a set of three was easiest to add?

• Did the child remember to add the third number to the sum of the pair?

• Was the child able to perform the computation mentally?

✦ **Make Up and Solve Number Stories Involving Addition, Subtraction, Equal Groups, Equal Sharing, or Equal Grouping**

As children write, illustrate, and solve number stories, you may want to use the sample rubric shown on page 57 for Lesson 6.4. You may also choose to compile children's number stories into books. Questions that you might consider as you assess children's progress include the following:

• Was the number story complete—was information given and a question posed?

• Did the number story ask a question that could be answered from the information given?

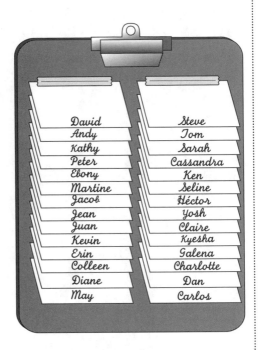

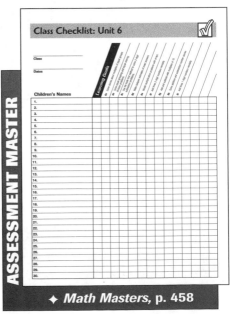

Class Checklist: Unit 6

Class

Dates

Children's Names

Learning Goals

✦ *Math Masters*, p. 458

ASSESSMENT MASTER

Unit 7
Assessment Overview

The focus of this unit is on patterns and rules. With the exception of Goal 7h in the chart below, the Secure goals are assessed using written, oral, and slate assessments (see Goals 7f–j on page 61). Many of the units also review skills introduced in earlier units. In this unit, for example, there are two important Developing/Secure goals (Goals 7d and 7e in the chart below) that deal with children's ability to measure to the nearest inch and to the nearest centimeter.

Ongoing Assessment Opportunities

Ongoing assessment opportunities are opportunities to observe children during regular interactions, as they work independently and in groups. You can conduct ongoing assessment during teacher-guided instruction, Math Boxes sessions, mathematical mini-interviews, games, Mental Math and Reflexes sessions, strategy sharing, and slate work. The chart below provides a summary of ongoing assessment opportunities in Unit 7, as they relate to specific Unit 7 learning goals.

7d **Developing/Secure Goal** Measure to the nearest inch. (Lessons 7.2 and 7.7)	Lesson 7.2, p. 520
7e **Developing/Secure Goal** Measure to the nearest centimeter. (Lessons 7.2 and 7.7)	Lesson 7.2, p. 520
7h **Secure Goal** Find missing addends for the next multiple of 10. (Lessons 7.2, 7.3, and 7.5)	Lesson 7.3, p. 525 Lesson 7.5, p. 536

Product Assessment Opportunities

Math Journals, Math Boxes, activity sheets, masters, Math Logs, and the results of Explorations and Projects all provide product assessment opportunities. On the next page is an example of how you might use a rubric to assess children's understanding of doubling and halving.

Lesson 7.10, p. 566

ALTERNATIVE ASSESSMENT Write a Doubles or Halves Story

Circulate around the room as children work independently to draw a picture of an imaginary animal or object that doubles or divides in half every hour. After children write short stories about their drawings, create a rubric or use the sample rubric below to evaluate their work.

Sample Rubric
Beginning (B) The child draws a picture of an animal or object, but it isn't obvious that it doubles or divides in half every hour. The story lacks an explanation of how the number of animals or objects increases with doubling, or there is no clear idea of what doubling means.
Developing (D) The child is able to make a distinctive drawing of an object or animal that doubles or divides in half, but has some difficulty describing the implications of this in his or her short story. For example, following the first doubling, the child might not be able to indicate in writing what happens after the animal or object doubles again.
Secure (S) The child successfully makes a drawing of an animal or object in which it is obvious that it has doubled or divided in half (or was capable of doing so). The story also indicates the child's grasp of the implications of doubling or halving every hour. For example, the child might mention that after one hour, there were two animals; after two hours, four; and so on.

Periodic Assessment Opportunities

Here is a summary of the periodic assessment opportunities that are provided in Unit 7. Refer to Lesson 7.10 for details.

Oral and Slate Assessment

In Lesson 7.10, you will find oral and slate assessment problems on pages 563–565.

Written Assessment

In Lesson 7.10, you will find written assessment problems on pages 565 and 566 (*Math Masters,* pages 429 and 430).

See the chart on the next page to find oral, slate, and written assessment problems that address specific learning goals.

7a	**Developing Goal** Find missing addends for any multiple of 10. (Lesson 7.3)	Slate Assessment, Problem 5 Written Assessment, Problem 2
7b	**Developing Goal** Find the median (middle value) of a data set. (Lesson 7.8)	Slate Assessment, Problem 7 Written Assessment, Problem 3
7c	**Developing Goal** Add three 2-digit numbers mentally. (Lesson 7.4)	Slate Assessment, Problem 6 Written Assessment, Problem 4
7d	**Developing/Secure Goal** Measure to the nearest inch. (Lessons 7.2 and 7.7)	Written Assessment, Problem 5
7e	**Developing/Secure Goal** Measure to the nearest centimeter. (Lessons 7.2 and 7.7)	Written Assessment, Problem 6
7f	**Secure Goal** Know complements of 10. (Lesson 7.3)	Slate Assessment, Problem 3
7g	**Secure Goal** Count by 2s, 5s, and 10s and describe the patterns. (Lesson 7.1)	Oral Assessment, Problem 1
7h	**Secure Goal** Find missing addends for the next multiple of 10. (Lessons 7.2, 7.3, and 7.5)	Slate Assessment, Problem 4 Written Assessment, Problem 1
7i	**Secure Goal** Solve number-grid puzzles. (Lesson 7.2)	Written Assessment, Problem 7
7j	**Secure Goal** Plot data on a bar graph. (Lesson 7.9)	Home Link 7.9 Follow-Up (*Math Masters,* page 138)

Alternative Assessment

In Lesson 7.10, you will find alternative assessment options on page 566.

✦ Play *Hit the Target*

Have children play *Hit the Target,* a game that was introduced in Lesson 7.3. Circulate and assess their ability to find the difference between 2-digit numbers and any higher multiple of 10. Children's record sheets from this game can also be used to assess their progress. Keep the following question in mind:

• Did the child find the difference in one step, or did he or she begin by finding the next-higher multiple of 10?

✦ Play *Basketball Addition*

Have children play *Basketball Addition,* a game that was introduced in Lesson 7.4. Circulate and assess children's ability to add three or more 1- and 2-digit numbers. Children's record sheets from this game also can be used to assess their progress. The following questions might also be helpful:

• Was the child able to find which pair of numbers in a set of three was easiest to add?

• Did the child remember to add the third number to the sum of the pair?

• Was the child able to perform the computation mentally?

✦ Write a Doubles or Halves Story

Suggestions for assessing this activity, including a sample scoring rubric, are given on page 60 in the Product Assessment Opportunities section. As an alternative, you might consider the following questions:

• Was the number story complete—was information given and a question posed?

• Did the number story ask a question that could be answered from the information given?

• Did the number story reflect understanding of doubling or halving?

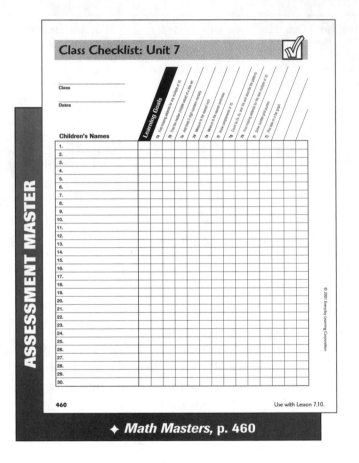

✦ *Math Masters, p. 460*

Unit 8
Assessment Overview

In this unit, children develop the important ability to work with fractions. Depending on the specific skill, children's ability levels might range from Beginning/Developing to Secure. Ongoing assessment opportunities are provided for three of the Developing goals (Goals 8b, 8c, and 8e in the chart below), whereas oral, slate, and written assessments must be used to assess the other goals (see the goal chart on page 65).

Ongoing Assessment Opportunities

Ongoing assessment opportunities are opportunities to observe children during regular interactions, as they work independently and in groups. You can conduct ongoing assessment during teacher-guided instruction, Math Boxes sessions, mathematical mini-interviews, games, Mental Math and Reflexes sessions, strategy sharing, and slate work. The chart below provides a summary of ongoing assessment opportunities in Unit 8, as they relate to specific Unit 8 learning goals.

8b **Developing Goal** Understand fractions as names for equal parts of a region or set. (Lessons 8.1–8.3 and 8.7)	Lesson 8.3, p. 592
8c **Developing Goal** Understand that the amount represented by a fraction depends on the size of the whole (or the ONE). (Lessons 8.2, 8.3, and 8.7)	Lesson 8.7, p. 607
8e **Developing Goal** Give the fraction name for the shaded part of a set. (Lesson 8.3)	Lesson 8.3, p. 592

Product Assessment Opportunities

Math Journals, Math Boxes, activity sheets, masters, Math Logs, and the results of Explorations and Projects all provide product assessment opportunities. Here is an example of how you might use a rubric to assess children's understanding of fractions greater than one.

Lesson 8.8, p. 613

ALTERNATIVE ASSESSMENT **Describe Fractions Greater Than ONE**

Children are asked to respond in writing to the following question: *Can fractions name things that are more or bigger than ONE? Give two examples. Draw a picture of one of your examples.* The sample rubric below can help you evaluate children's work.

Sample Rubric

Beginning (B)
Either the child answers that fractions cannot name things that are more than ONE or responds with an incorrect example. For example, the child may indicate that fractions like $\frac{3}{4}$ or $\frac{2}{3}$ are more than ONE. The child might also write that $\frac{1}{4}$ of a pizza and another $\frac{1}{4}$ of the pizza is more than ONE.

Developing (D)
The child is able to provide at least one correct example, but the second example is incorrect. Or the child provides correct examples without appropriate drawings to accompany them. For instance, one of the examples might describe $1\frac{1}{2}$ cookies, but the illustration may show only two half-cookies.

Secure (S)
The child is able to provide at least two correct examples of fractions that are greater than ONE, along with illustrations that correctly represent the example numerically. For instance, the child's example might indicate $1\frac{1}{2}$ cookies, along with a sketch of three half-cookies.

Periodic Assessment Opportunities

Here is a summary of the periodic assessment opportunities that are provided in Unit 8. Refer to Lesson 8.8 for details.

Oral and Slate Assessment

In Lesson 8.8, you will find oral and slate assessment problems on pages 611 and 612.

Written Assessment

In Lesson 8.8, you will find written assessment problems on page 612 (*Math Masters,* page 431).

See the chart on the next page to find oral, slate, and written assessment problems that address specific learning goals.

8a	**Beginning/Developing Goal** Compare fractions less than one. (Lessons 8.5–8.7)	Oral Assessment, Problem 6
8b	**Developing Goal** Understand fractions as names for equal parts of a region or set. (Lessons 8.1–8.3 and 8.7)	Oral Assessment, Problems 1 and 2 Slate Assessment, Problems 1 and 2 Written Assessment, Problem 1
8c	**Developing Goal** Understand that the amount represented by a fraction depends on the size of the whole (or the ONE). (Lessons 8.2, 8.3, and 8.7)	Oral Assessment, Problems 1, 2, and 4 Slate Assessment, Problem 3
8d	**Developing Goal** Shade a specified fractional part of a set. (Lessons 8.3–8.5)	Written Assessment, Problems 8 and 9
8e	**Developing Goal** Give the fraction name for the shaded part of a set. (Lesson 8.3)	Written Assessment, Problems 2 and 5
8f	**Developing Goal** Find equivalent fractions for given fractions. (Lessons 8.4–8.6)	Oral Assessment, Problems 3 and 5
8g	**Developing Goal** Shade a specified fractional part of a region. (Lessons 8.1–8.4)	Written Assessment, Problems 6 and 7
8h	**Developing Goal** Give the fraction name for the shaded part of a region. (Lessons 8.1, 8.3, and 8.5)	Slate Assessment, Problem 3 Written Assessment, Problems 1, 3, and 4

Alternative Assessment

In Lesson 8.8, you will find alternative assessment options on pages 613 and 614.

✦ Name Fractional Parts of a Region

Children draw a design, using one of the shapes on a Pattern-Block Template. The design represents the ONE. Then children write what fraction each part of the design represents. Circulate and consider the following questions as you assess their progress:

• Was the shape divided into equal parts?

• Was the child able to correctly identify the fraction that each part of the shape represented?

✦ Describe Fractions Greater Than ONE

The following question is asked of children: *Can fractions name things that are more or bigger than ONE? Give two examples. Draw a picture of one of your examples.* To assess children's understanding, use the sample rubric from page 64 in the Product Assessment Opportunities section. As an alternative, consider the following questions:

• Did the child understand fractions greater than ONE?

• Did the child's diagrams accurately represent the fractions that he or she names?

✦ **Math Masters, p. 462**

✦ Write and Solve Number Stories Involving Fractions

Children solve number stories, either those that you generate or those that children themselves generate. Consider the following questions as you assess their understanding:

• Did the child understand the fractions named in the number story?

• Did the number stories written by the child correctly include fractions?

• Did the child understand the concept of the "ONE" as it is related to fractions?

✦ Play the *Equivalent Fractions* Game or *Fraction Top-It*

As children play these games, circulate and assess their ability to compare fractions. Consider the following questions:

• Was the child able to find pairs of equivalent fractions?

• Was the child able to recognize whether a fraction is larger than, smaller than, or equivalent to other fractions?

• Was the child able to accomplish this task with or without the aid of a region model?

Unit 9
Assessment Overview

In this unit, children develop their abilities to measure, to use appropriate units for measurement, and to find perimeter and area. Depending on the particular goal, ability levels should range from Beginning/Developing to Secure. Suggestions for ongoing assessment can be found in the goal chart below. Refer to the charts on pages 68 and 69 for oral, slate, and written assessment suggestions.

At this stage of the *Second Grade Everyday Mathematics* program, you might reflect on your success in developing a balanced assessment plan. Think about how your plan could be improved in preparation for next year.

Ongoing Assessment Opportunities

Ongoing assessment opportunities are opportunities to observe children during regular interactions, as they work independently and in groups. You can conduct ongoing assessment during teacher-guided instruction, Math Boxes sessions, mathematical mini-interviews, games, Mental Math and Reflexes sessions, strategy sharing, and slate work. The chart below provides a summary of ongoing assessment opportunities in Unit 9, as they relate to specific Unit 9 learning goals.

9d	**Developing Goal** Use appropriate units for measurement and recognize sensible measurements. (Lessons 9.1–9.6, 9.9, and 9.10)	Lesson 9.1, p. 634 Lesson 9.6, p. 659
9h	**Developing/Secure Goal** Use a ruler, tape measure, and meter/yardstick correctly. (Lessons 9.1–9.4)	Lesson 9.1, p. 634

Product Assessment Opportunities

Math Journals, Math Boxes, activity sheets, masters, Math Logs, and the results of Explorations and Projects all provide product assessment opportunities. On the next page is an example of how you might use a rubric to assess children's ability to measure to the nearest half-inch and half-centimeter.

EXTRA PRACTICE Measuring to the Nearest Half-Inch and Half-Centimeter

Children practice measuring objects in the classroom to the nearest half-inch and half-centimeter. They also draw a picture of each item and indicate which part they measured. The sample rubric that follows can help you evaluate children's measuring skills.

Portfolio Ideas

Sample Rubric

Beginning (B)
The child has much difficulty getting started with this activity. He or she may try to measure an object using a ruler incorrectly, by, for example, not starting at 0. The child also needs assistance reading the ruler to the nearest half-inch or half-centimeter. He or she may attempt to draw the object, along with the part that is measured.

Developing (D)
The child is able to start the measurement activity without teacher assistance. He or she can use the ruler correctly but still needs assistance reading the ruler to the nearest half-inch or half-centimeter. A picture of each item measured is drawn, along with the part that is measured.

Secure (S)
The child has much success completing the measurement activity independently. The objects selected are measured correctly using the ruler and are measured to the nearest half-inch or half-centimeter. A picture of each item measured is drawn, along with the part that is measured.

Periodic Assessment Opportunities

Here is a summary of the periodic assessment opportunities that are provided in Unit 9. Refer to Lesson 9.11 for details.

Oral and Slate Assessment

In Lesson 9.11, you will find oral and slate assessment problems on pages 684 and 685.

Written Assessment

In Lesson 9.11, you will find written assessment problems on page 685 (*Math Masters*, page 432).

See the chart below and on the next page to find oral, slate, and written assessment problems that address specific learning goals.

9a	**Beginning/Developing Goal** Identify equivalencies for mm, cm, dm, and m. (Lessons 9.2, 9.3, 9.5, and 9.9)	Slate Assessment, Problem 2
9b	**Developing Goal** Measure to the nearest $\frac{1}{2}$ inch. (Lesson 9.3)	Written Assessment, Problems 1 and 2
9c	**Developing Goal** Measure to the nearest $\frac{1}{2}$ cm. (Lesson 9.3)	Written Assessment, Problem 3
9d	**Developing Goal** Use appropriate units for measurement and recognize sensible measurements. (Lessons 9.1–9.6, 9.9, and 9.10)	Oral Assessment, Problems 1–3, 6, and 7 Written Assessment, Problems 5 and 6

9e	**Developing Goal** Find area concretely. (Lessons 9.7 and 9.8)	Written Assessment, Problems 7 and 8
9f	**Developing Goal** Find perimeter concretely. (Lessons 9.4, 9.5, and 9.8)	Written Assessment, Problems 4, 7, and 8
9g	**Developing Goal** Identify equivalencies for inches, feet, and yards. (Lessons 9.2 and 9.9)	Slate Assessment, Problem 1
9h	**Developing/Secure Goal** Use a ruler, tape measure, and meter/yardstick correctly. (Lessons 9.1–9.4)	Written Assessment, Problems 1–3

Alternative Assessment

In Lesson 9.11, you will find alternative assessment options on page 686.

✦ Complete a Missing Measurements Story

Use this activity to assess children's understanding of reasonable measurements using a variety of measurement units. Keep the following questions in mind as you assess children's progress:

• Did the child record measurements that corresponded to the appropriate measurement unit?

• Was the child able to change the information once the story was read so that the story made sense?

✦ Construct a Display of Fish Lengths

Assess children's ability to use a tape measure and yardstick by observing them as they measure strings that match the lengths of the fish given on the Fish Poster. As you circulate, use a Class Checklist or Flip Cards to record children's progress. Keep the following questions in mind:

• Was the child able to make accurate measurements using the tape measure and yardstick?

• Was the child able to order the strings from shortest to longest?

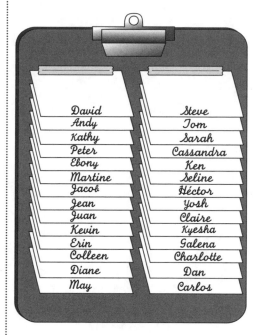

Class Checklist: Unit 9

✦ *Math Masters, p. 464*

ASSESSMENT MASTER

Unit 10
Assessment Overview

By this time, perhaps you have tried several different types of assessment strategies. Remember, as you use a balance of assessment approaches, the overall effectiveness of your assessment plan should improve. If there is still a major type of assessment, such as Ongoing, Product, or Periodic, that you haven't used, this unit might be a good time to try it.

Ongoing Assessment Opportunities

Ongoing assessment opportunities are opportunities to observe children during regular interactions, as they work independently and in groups. You can conduct ongoing assessment during teacher-guided instruction, Math Boxes sessions, mathematical mini-interviews, games, Mental Math and Reflexes sessions, strategy sharing, and slate work. The chart below provides a summary of ongoing assessment opportunities in Unit 10, as they relate to specific Unit 10 learning goals.

10b **Developing Goal** Solve money stories involving change. (Lessons 10.6 and 10.8)	Lesson 10.6, p. 725
10c **Developing Goal** Estimate totals for "ballpark" check of exact answers. (Lessons 10.5, 10.6, 10.8, and 10.9)	Lesson 10.6, p. 725
10e **Developing/Secure Goal** Read and write money amounts in decimal notation. (Lessons 10.2–10.4 and 10.6)	Lesson 10.2, p. 712 Lesson 10.6, p. 725
10f **Secure Goal** Use equivalent coins to show money amounts in different ways. (Lesson 10.1)	Lesson 10.1, p. 701
10g **Secure Goal** Use a calculator to compute money amounts. (Lessons 10.2, 10.3, 10.4 and 10.7)	Lesson 10.2, p. 712

Product Assessment Opportunities

Math Journals, Math Boxes, activity sheets, masters, Math Logs, and the results of Explorations and Projects all provide product assessment opportunities. On the next page is an example of how you might use a rubric to assess children's ability to write number stories.

Lesson 10.12, p. 756
ALTERNATIVE ASSESSMENT Write Number Stories

Children write number stories that require finding the total cost of several items. Each story should also include the amount of change owed after the purchase. Children focus on writing a number story that contains all necessary parts: unit, picture, number model, and a question/answer. Provide *Math Masters,* page 22 from Unit 2 on which children create their number stories. The sample rubric that follows can help you evaluate children's work.

Portfolio
Ideas

Sample Rubric
Beginning (B) The child needs assistance in getting started with the number story. The story is incomplete. The child may attempt to write a story that involves money, but it does not require finding a total. Most of the components for a number story are missing.
Developing (D) The child attempts to write and solve a number story, without teacher assistance, that involves money. The story requires finding a total cost of several items. One or more elements of a number story—unit, picture, number model, and question/answer—are missing or poorly done.
Secure (S) The child writes a number story, without teacher assistance, that requires finding the total cost of several items. The story contains all or most of the following components: unit, picture, number model, and question/answer. The question is answered correctly. The child may also include the amount of change owed after the purchase.

Periodic Assessment Opportunities

Here is a summary of the periodic assessment opportunities that are provided in Unit 10. Refer to Lesson 10.12 for details.

Oral and Slate Assessment

In Lesson 10.12, you will find oral and slate assessment problems on pages 753 and 754.

Written Assessment

In Lesson 10.12, you will find written assessment problems on page 755 (*Math Masters,* pages 433 and 434).

See the chart below and on the next page to find oral, slate, and written assessment problems that address specific learning goals.

10a	**Beginning Goal** Use parentheses in number models. (Lesson 10.11)	Slate Assessment, Problems 5 and 6
10b	**Developing Goal** Solve money stories involving change. (Lessons 10.6 and 10.8)	Written Assessment, Problem 9
10c	**Developing Goal** Estimate totals for "ballpark" check of exact answers. (Lessons 10.5, 10.6, 10.8, and 10.9)	Written Assessment, Problems 8 and 9
10d	**Developing Goal** Know and express automatically the values of digits in 5-digit numbers. (Lessons 10.10 and 10.11)	Written Assessment, Problems 11–14

10e	**Developing/Secure Goal** Read and write money amounts in decimal notation. (Lessons 10.2–10.4 and 10.6)	Oral Assessment, Problem 2 Slate Assessment, Problems 1 and 3 Written Assessment, Problem 1
10f	**Secure Goal** Use equivalent coins to show money amounts in different ways. (Lesson 10.1)	Written Assessment, Problem 2
10g	**Secure Goal** Use a calculator to compute money amounts. (Lessons 10.3, 10.4, and 10.7)	Slate Assessment, Problem 4 Written Assessment, Problems 8 and 9
10h	**Secure Goal** Exchange pennies, nickels, dimes, and quarters. (Lessons 10.2, 10.8, and 10.10)	Written Assessment, Problems 3–7
10i	**Developing/Secure Goal** Know and express automatically the values of digits in 2-, 3-, and 4-digit numbers. (Lessons 10.8–10.11)	Oral Assessment, Problem 1 Slate Assessment, Problem 2 Written Assessment, Problems 10 and 12

Alternative Assessment

In Lesson 10.12, you will find alternative assessment options on pages 755 and 756.

✦ Write about Mathematics

Use this activity to assess children's flexibility in mathematical thinking. They respond to the following statement: Someone said that a 5 is a 5, no matter what. Is that always true? Give examples. Assess children, keeping the following questions in mind:

• Did the child give just one or two examples as to why 5 is not always 5, or many different examples?

• Was the child clearly able to articulate his or her thinking through writing?

✦ Write Number Stories

See the suggestions and rubric given in Product Assessment Opportunities on pages 70 and 71 of this book.

✦ Play *Pick-a-Coin*

As children play this game from Lesson 10.3, assess their understanding of how to enter amounts of money into the calculator. Observe the strategies children are using when placing the numbers in the columns. This is a good opportunity for children to estimate before finding the total.

✦ Play *Spinning for Money*

As children play this game from Lessons 3.2 and 10.1, evaluate their understanding of how to exchange coins of lesser value for a single coin or bill of greater value. This is also a good opportunity to observe children's money-counting skills.

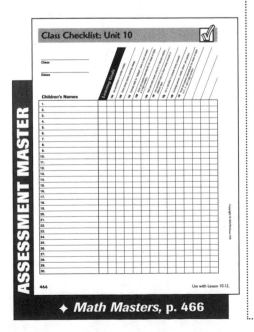

David   Steve
Andy   Tom
Kathy   Sarah
Peter   Cassandra
Ebony   Ken
Martine   Seline
Jacob   Héctor
Jean   Yosh
Juan   Claire
Kevin   Kyesha
Erin   Galena
Colleen   Charlotte
Diane   Dan
May   Carlos

ASSESSMENT MASTER

Class Checklist: Unit 10

Class

Dates

Learning Goals

Children's Names

466   Use with Lesson 10.12.

✦ *Math Masters*, p. 466

Unit 11
Assessment Overview

As you near the end of the *Second Grade Everyday Mathematics* program, you might want to think about which assessment strategies worked best. Also, are there strategies that you did not have time to try this year, but that you would like to try next year? To help you remember them next fall, record your thoughts on the note pages in this book.

Ongoing Assessment Opportunities

Ongoing assessment opportunities are opportunities to observe children during regular interactions, as they work independently and in groups. You can conduct ongoing assessment during teacher-guided instruction, Math Boxes sessions, mathematical mini-interviews, games, Mental Math and Reflexes sessions, strategy sharing, and slate work. The chart below provides a summary of ongoing assessment opportunities in Unit 11, as they relate to specific Unit 11 learning goals.

11d	**Developing Goal** Multiply numbers with 2, 5, or 10 as a factor. (Lessons 11.5–11.9)	Lesson 11.7, p. 810 Lesson 11.8, p. 814
11g	**Developing/Secure Goal** Multiply numbers with 0 or 1 as a factor. (Lessons 11.6–11.8)	Lesson 11.7, p. 810 Lesson 11.8, p. 814

Product Assessment Opportunities

Math Journals, Math Boxes, activity sheets, masters, Math Logs, and the results of Explorations and Projects all provide product assessment opportunities. On the next page is an example of how you might use a rubric to assess children's ability to make up and solve multiplication and division number stories.

Lesson 11.7, p. 811

ENRICHMENT **Making Up and Solving Multiplication and Division Number Stories**

Children write and solve multiplication and division number stories. They should also focus on writing a number story that contains all necessary parts: unit, picture, number model, and question/answer. The sample rubric below can help you evaluate children's work. These number stories can be compiled into a book and used throughout the year for children to refer to. Children can use *Math Masters*, page 22 to record number stories.

Sample Rubric
Beginning (B)   The child needs assistance in getting started. The number story is incomplete. The story may not be connected to multiplication or division. For example, the child may write an addition number story for 4×5, instead of a story talking about 4 groups of 5. The child does not include most of the number-story components.
Developing (D)   The child attempts to write a number story without teacher assistance. The story is connected to multiplication or division, and it contains some, but not all, of the number-story components.
Secure (S)   The child writes a number story without teacher assistance that contains all of the following components: unit, picture, number model, and question. The story is connected to multiplication or division and is answered correctly.

Periodic Assessment Opportunities

Here is a summary of the periodic assessment opportunities that are provided in Unit 11. Refer to Lesson 11.10 for details.

Oral and Slate Assessment

In Lesson 11.10, you will find oral and slate assessment problems on pages 822 and 823.

Written Assessment

In Lesson 11.10, you will find written assessment problems on page 824 (*Math Masters*, page 435).

See the chart below and on the next page to find oral, slate, and written assessment problems that address specific learning goals.

11a **Developing Goal** Estimate and solve addition and subtraction number stories with dollars and cents. (Lessons 11.1 and 11.2)	Oral Assessment,
	   Problems 1 and 2
	 Written Assessment,
	   Problems 1–3

11b **Developing Goal** Solve 1-digit multiplication stories (multiples of equal groups). (Lessons 11.3 and 11.7)	Slate Assessment, Problem 2 Written Assessment, Problems 4, 5, 6, and 8
11c **Developing Goal** Solve equal grouping and equal sharing division stories. (Lessons 11.4 and 11.7)	Slate Assessment, Problem 3 Written Assessment, Problem 8

11d **Developing Goal** Multiply numbers with 2, 5, or 10 as a factor. (Lessons 11.5–11.9)	Slate Assessment, Problem 1	
11e **Developing Goal** Complete multiplication/division fact families. (Lessons 11.7 and 11.8)	Written Assessment, Problem 7	
11f **Developing Goal** Make difference and ratio comparisons. (Lessons 11.2 and 11.9)	Slate Assessment, Problem 4	
11g **Developing/Secure Goal** Multiply numbers with 0 or 1 as a factor. (Lessons 11.6–11.8)	Slate Assessment, Problem 1	

Alternative Assessment

In Lesson 11.10, you will find alternative assessment options on pages 824 and 825.

✦ Write about Mathematics

Use this independent activity to assess children's thinking about multiplication. Children are asked to draw a diagram or picture to show how $3 + 3 + 3 + 3 + 3 + 3 + 3$ is similar to 7×3. Assess their work and keep the following questions in mind:

- Did the child draw a picture that illustrates $3 + 3 + 3 + 3 + 3 + 3 + 3$ and one that illustrates 7×3? Do they look the same?

- Did both pictures represent 7 groups of 3?

- Did the child realize that both pictures show 21?

- Was the child able to write a few sentences explaining why the two number models are similar?

✦ Make Up and Solve Addition, Subtraction, Multiplication, and Division Number Stories

Children work in pairs to make up an addition, a subtraction, and a multiplication number story, using *Math Masters,* page 201. They should focus on using the toys and money amounts given on the Museum Store Poster. Children can use *Math Masters,* page 22 from previous units to record the number stories. Consider making number storybooks that children can use for extra practice or review. Collect the number stories and keep such questions as the following in mind as you assess progress:

- Did the story involve the operation that is shown by the number model? In other words, did the number story go with the number model?

- Were the partners able to come up with a number story for each of the three operations listed (addition, subtraction, and multiplication)?

- Were there any children who seem ready for the challenge of writing a division number story?

- Did the number stories use all of the necessary components (unit, picture, number model, and question/answer)?

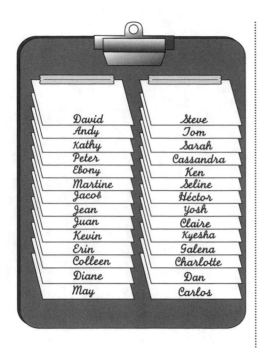

✦ Play *Beat the Calculator*

Use this game from Lesson 11.8 to assess children's multiplication-fact automaticity. Children use journal pages 292 and 293 to record check marks each time they beat the calculator. Three check marks indicate fact automaticity. As children play the game in groups of three, circulate using the Class Checklist or Flip Cards to record their progress. Children can also record, on a half-sheet of paper, the facts for which they can beat the calculator.

✦ Practice Multiplication Facts with Fact Triangles

As children work in pairs to practice their facts, record their progress using a Class Checklist or Flip Cards. Children can also use the Fact Triangles in this activity to sort into two piles the facts they know and the facts they still need to practice. After children complete the sorting, ask them to record on a sheet of paper the facts they still need to practice. These sheets can be sent home as a reference to parents so that they can help children with their multiplication facts.

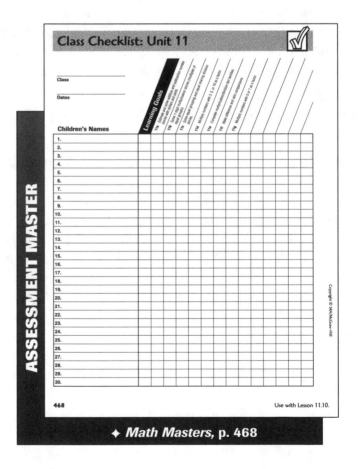

✦ *Math Masters*, p. 468

Unit 12
Assessment Overview

Looking back over the *Second Grade Everyday Mathematics* program, have you been able to establish a balance of Ongoing, Product, and Periodic Assessment strategies? Have your strategies included both anecdotal records based on observations of children's progress and the use of written assessments? This might be a good time to evaluate your assessment strategies and think about approaches you might consider for next year.

Ongoing Assessment Opportunities

Ongoing assessment opportunities are opportunities to observe children during regular interactions, as they work independently and in groups. You can conduct ongoing assessment during teacher-guided instruction, Math Boxes sessions, mathematical mini-interviews, games, Mental Math and Reflexes sessions, strategy sharing, and slate work. The chart below provides a summary of ongoing assessment opportunities in Unit 12, as they relate to specific Unit 12 learning goals.

12b **Beginning Goal** Know multiplication facts. (Lessons 12.4 and 12.5)	Lesson 12.4, p. 851
12f **Developing/Secure Goal** Multiply numbers with 2, 5, and 10 as a factor. (Lesson 12.4)	Lesson 12.4, p. 851

Product Assessment Opportunities

Math Journals, Math Boxes, activity sheets, masters, Math Logs, and the results of Explorations and Projects all provide product assessment opportunities. On the next page is an example of how you might use a rubric to assess children's ability to construct a timeline.

Lesson 12.3, p. 848

ENRICHMENT Creating a Timeline of a Person's Life

Children are asked to create a timeline to display the important events of a family member's or an important person's life. Then, children share their timelines with the class. The sample rubric below can help you evaluate children's understanding of timelines.

Sample Rubric

Beginning (B)
The child needs assistance getting started. For example, he or she may have difficulty arranging the events in sequential order. The timeline may not be divided into equal intervals, such as decades. The child may require additional assistance in locating the dots for events at the proper position between major intervals. He or she has difficulty either estimating distance between intervals (in other words, a dot for "1986" might be closer to 1980 than to 1990), or else cannot identify the correct interval in which to place the dot.

Developing (D)
The child attempts to construct a timeline without teacher assistance, and represents events in sequential order. The child may experience some difficulty in dividing the timeline into equal and useful intervals. Once this is achieved, the child locates the dots properly with little assistance.

Secure (S)
The child constructs a timeline correctly, using meaningful intervals of time. Then he or she correctly locates the dots for important events on the timeline.

Periodic Assessment Opportunities

Here is a summary of the periodic assessment opportunities that are provided for Unit 12. Refer to Lesson 12.8 for details.

Oral and Slate Assessment

In Lesson 12.8, you will find oral and slate assessment problems on pages 870 and 871.

Written Assessment

In Lesson 12.8, you will find written assessment problems on pages 871 and 872 (*Math Masters,* pages 436 and 437).

See the chart below and on the next page to find oral, slate, and written assessment problems that address specific learning goals.

12a	**Beginning Goal** Use alternative names for times. (Lesson 12.2)	Oral Assessment, Problem 1
12b	**Beginning Goal** Know multiplication facts. (Lessons 12.4 and 12.5)	Slate Assessment, Problem 1
12c	**Beginning/Developing Goal** Determine the mode of a data set. (Lesson 12.7)	Slate Assessment, Problem 4 Written Assessment, Problem 21
12d	**Developing Goal** Determine the median, maximum, minimum, and range of a data set. (Lessons 12.6 and 12.7)	Slate Assessment, Problem 4 Written Assessment, Problems 17–19

12e **Developing/Secure Goal** Complete multiplication/ division fact families. (Lessons 12.1 and 12.5)	Slate Assessment, Problem 3 Written Assessment, Problem 7
12f **Developing/Secure Goal** Multiply numbers with 2, 5, and 10 as a factor. (Lesson 12.4)	Written Assessment, Problems 8–16
12g **Secure Goal** Tell time to 5-minute intervals. (Lessons 12.1 and 12.2)	Written Assessment, Problems 1–6
12h **Secure Goal** Demonstrate calendar concepts and skills. (Lesson 12.1)	Oral Assessment, Problems 2 and 3 Slate Assessment, Problem 2
12i **Secure Goal** Compare quantities from a bar graph. (Lessons 12.6 and 12.7)	Written Assessment, Problem 20

Alternative Assessment

In Lesson 12.8, you will find alternative assessment options on page 872.

✦ Practice Multiplication Facts with Fact Triangle Cards

Circulate as children sort their triangles into two piles—facts they know and facts they still need to practice. After children record the facts that they need to practice on a sheet of paper, collect the facts as a record of their progress. As you circulate through the classroom, keep the following questions in mind:

• Did children honestly sort their triangles, in other words, did they actually know the facts for those triangles they placed into the "know" file?

• Were there certain facts that most children had difficulty with?

✦ Play *Clock Concentration*

Circulate and assess children's progress as they play the advanced version of *Clock Concentration.* Keep questions such as the following in mind:

• Did children correctly write alternative names for the times they drew on their clock faces? For example, if a clock read "six fifteen," did the child write "quarter-past six," or "fifteen after six," or did he or she incorrectly write "half-past six" or another incorrect time?

• Did children's responses during the game demonstrate their ability to tell time correctly?

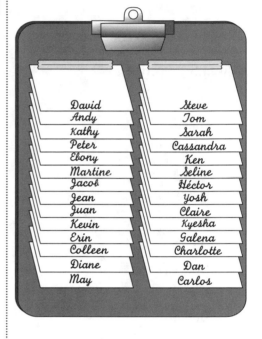

✦ *Math Masters*, p. 470

ASSESSMENT MASTER

Assessment Masters

How to Use the Masters

The *Assessment Handbook* contains reduced versions of all of the Assessment Masters found in your *Math Masters* book. You can use these reduced pages to assist you in programming your assessment plan. The following general masters may be adapted in any way to suit your needs; however, the suggestions below may be helpful.

Use the **List of Assessment Sources** to keep track of the sources that you are currently using. As you plan your assessment, aim for the balance of techniques that will meet your children's needs.

On the **Individual Profile of Progress**

- Copy the Learning Goals from the Assessment Lesson at the end of each unit. (See the *Teacher's Lesson Guide.*)
- Make as many copies of the form as you need for each child in your class.
- Keep track of each child's progress on each unit's skills and concepts using this form.
- Check whether each child is Beginning, Developing, or Secure in each of the content areas.
- You may alternatively wish to use the **Class Checklist.**

Make several copies of the **Class Progress Indicator.** Use one page for each mathematical topic being assessed. Fill in the topic you wish to assess under the chart heading and then write each child's name in the appropriate box, indicating whether he or she is Beginning, Developing, or Secure.

The **Parent Reflections** master can be sent to parents prior to parent-teacher conferences, so that parents can identify their concerns prior to the meeting.

You can use the **Rubric** master to create your own rubric for a given task, especially for products that will be included in portfolios. Use Beginning, Developing, Secure or your own rubric scheme.

All of the other forms are to be passed out to children. Use the interest inventories to find out how children feel about mathematics. Self-assessment forms should be used as attachments to portfolio items. The remaining forms can provide insight into how comfortable children feel with the math content.

> NOTE: This page provides a brief summary of how the general Assessment Masters may be used. The uses of these masters are described in more detail near the front of this book on pages 5–33.

Unit 1 Checking Progress

Name _____ Date _____ Time _____

1. Show 17 with tally marks. _||||| ||||| ||_

2. Write the amount.

Total: $ _27_

3. Write the largest number you can with the digits 6, 3, and 9. Use each digit only once. _963_

4. Find each missing number.

$$4 + 6 = \boxed{10}$$

$$7 + \boxed{5} = 12$$

$$\boxed{3} + 5 = 8$$

5. Fill in the missing numbers.

| 87 | 88 | 89 | 90 |

| 79 |

| 79 | 89 |
| 99 | 100 |

6. Draw coins to show 35¢ two different ways. Use Ⓟ, Ⓝ, Ⓓ, and Ⓠ for coins. Sample answers:

ⓆⒹ   ⓃⓃⓃⓃⓃⓃⓃ

7. Write three different names for 20. Sample answers:

_5 + 5 + 10_   _veinte_   _21 − 1_

Use with Lesson 1.14.

419

Unit 2 Checking Progress

Name _____ Date _____ Time _____

1. Write the fact family for 2, 11, and 9.

$$2 + 9 = 11 \qquad 9 + 2 = 11$$
$$11 - 2 = 9 \qquad 11 - 9 = 2$$

2. Circle the names for 14.

(9 + 5)   7 − 3   (12 + 2)   (8 + 6)

1 + 11   (7 + 7)   3 + 9   (18 − 4)

5 + 6

3. Fill in the empty frames.

| 20 | 25 | 30 | 35 | 40 | 45 |

4. Find the rule and complete the table.

Rule: +6

in	out
9	15
6	12
4	10
7	13
10	16
8	14

Use with Lesson 2.14.

420

Name   Date   Time

Unit 3 Checking Progress

1. You buy a green pepper for 27¢. Write P, N, D, or Q to show the coins you could use to pay the exact amount.

Show coins one way.

Sample answer: 1 quarter and 2 pennies

Show coins another way.

Sample answer: 1 dime, 3 nickels, and 2 pennies

2. Fill in the frames.

Rule
Subtract 10

65 → 55 → 59 → 49 → 53 → 43

Rule
Add 4

3. Find the second rule. Fill in the frames.

Rule
Add 10¢

15¢ → 25¢ → 20¢ → 30¢ → 25¢ → 35¢

Rule
Subtract 5¢

Use with Lesson 3.9.

422

Name   Date   Time

Unit 2 Checking Progress (cont.)

5. Add.

a. $6 + 1 = \underline{7}$ **b.** $0 + 9 = \underline{9}$ **c.** $\underline{8} = 2 + 6$

d. $\begin{array}{r} 4 \\ +4 \\ \hline 8 \end{array}$ **e.** $\begin{array}{r} 3 \\ +5 \\ \hline 8 \end{array}$

6. Add.

a. $7 + 7 = \underline{14}$ **b.** $9 + 4 = \underline{13}$ **c.** $\underline{15} = 6 + 9$

d. $\begin{array}{r} 8 \\ +6 \\ \hline 14 \end{array}$ **e.** $\begin{array}{r} 5 \\ +7 \\ \hline 12 \end{array}$

7. Subtract.

a. $7 - 0 = \underline{7}$ **b.** $\underline{10} = 11 - 1$ **c.** $7 - 4 = \underline{3}$

d. $\begin{array}{r} 6 \\ -2 \\ \hline 4 \end{array}$ **e.** $\begin{array}{r} 9 \\ -5 \\ \hline 4 \end{array}$

8. Subtract.

a. $16 - 9 = \underline{7}$ **b.** $18 - 9 = \underline{9}$ **c.** $\underline{8} = 14 - 6$

d. $\begin{array}{r} 15 \\ -8 \\ \hline 7 \end{array}$ **e.** $\begin{array}{r} 13 \\ -5 \\ \hline 8 \end{array}$

Use with Lesson 2.14.

421

Name _____ Date _____ Time _____

Unit 4 Checking Progress

In the diagram for each number story:

- Write the numbers you know.
- Write ? for the number you want to find.
- Write the answer. Don't forget to include the unit.
- Write a number model.

1. Arlene has 20 dolls. Katie has 7 dolls. How many dolls do Arlene and Katie have in all?

Total	
?	
Part	Part
20	7

Answer: ___27 dolls___
(unit)

Number model: ___$20 + 7 = 27$___

2. On Monday, Jen painted 30 beads for her necklace. On Tuesday, she painted 12 beads. How many beads did Jen paint in all?

Total	
?	
Part	Part
30	12

Answer: ___42 beads___
(unit)

Number model: ___$30 + 12 = 42$___

3. At 2:30 in the afternoon, the temperature was 68°F. During the night, it went down 20 degrees. What was the new temperature?

Start	Change	End
68	−20	?

Answer: ___48°F___
(unit)

Number model: ___$68 - 20 = 48$ or $20 + 48 = 68$___

© 2001 Everyday Learning Corporation

Use with Lesson 4.10.

424

Name _____ Date _____ Time _____

Unit 3 Checking Progress (cont.)

4. You buy carrot juice for 60¢. You put 3 quarters in the vending machine. How much change should you receive? ___15¢___

5. You buy a head of lettuce for 68¢. You pay with a $1 bill. How much change should you receive? ___32¢___

6. Draw the hands to show 5:15.

7. Draw the hands to show 9:05.

8. Write the time.

3 : 20

9. Write the time.

7 : 50

© 2001 Everyday Learning Corporation

Use with Lesson 3.9.

423

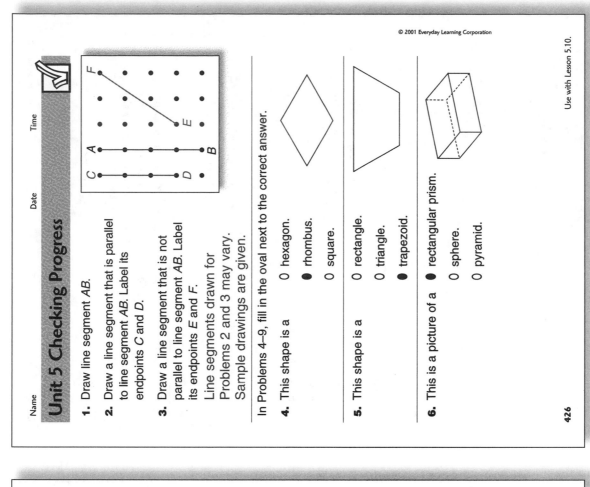

Unit 5 Checking Progress

Name   Date   Time

1. Draw line segment *AB*.

2. Draw a line segment that is parallel to line segment *AB*. Label its endpoints *C* and *D*.

3. Draw a line segment that is not parallel to line segment *AB*. Label its endpoints *E* and *F*.

   Line segments drawn for Problems 2 and 3 may vary. Sample drawings are given.

In Problems 4–9, fill in the oval next to the correct answer.

4. This shape is a
   - ○ hexagon.
   - ● rhombus.
   - ○ square.

5. This shape is a
   - ○ rectangle.
   - ○ triangle.
   - ● trapezoid.

6. This is a picture of a
   - ● rectangular prism.
   - ○ sphere.
   - ○ pyramid.

Use with Lesson 5.10.

426

Unit 4 Checking Progress (cont.)

Name   Date   Time

4. Kevin brought 36 cupcakes to school for his birthday. He gave 10 away during lunch. How many cupcakes did he have then?

Start	Change	End
36	−10	?

Answer: __26 cupcakes__
(unit)

Number model: __$36 - 10 = 26$ or $10 + 26 = 36$__

Write the temperature shown on each thermometer.

5. °F ... __62__ °F

6. °F ... __21__ °F

Mark each thermometer to show the temperature.

7. 30°F

8. 49°F

Solve the addition problems.

9. 53
   + 66

   119

10. 27
   + 48

   75

11. 34
   + 37

   71

12. 95
   + 63

   158

Use with Lesson 4.10.

425

Unit 6 Checking Progress

Name _____ Date _____ Time _____

1. Choose a unit. Solve the problems.

Unit ☐

$12 + 7 + 8 = $ __27__   __60__ $ = 24 + 30 + 6$

$33 = 13 + 9 + 11$ $17 + 12 + 33 = $ __62__

Subtract.

2.
$$\begin{array}{r} 78 \\ -52 \\ \hline 26 \end{array}$$

3.
$$\begin{array}{r} 64 \\ -29 \\ \hline 35 \end{array}$$

4.
$$\begin{array}{r} 83 \\ -59 \\ \hline 24 \end{array}$$

5.

How many rows? __4__

How many dots in each row? __7__

How many dots in all? __28__

Number model:

__4__ × __7__ = __28__

6. Draw an array with 3 rows and 5 dots in each row.

How many dots in all? __15__

Number model:

__3__ × __5__ = __15__

7. Fish J weighs 24 pounds. Fish H weighs 14 pounds. How much more does Fish J weigh?

__10__ pounds more

8. Fish K weighs 35 pounds. Fish G weighs 10 pounds. How much do they weigh together?

__45__ pounds

Use with Lesson 6.12.

428

Unit 5 Checking Progress (cont.)

Name _____ Date _____ Time _____

7. This is a picture of a
- ○ cylinder.
- ● cone.
- ○ sphere.

8. This is a picture of a
- ○ cylinder.
- ● pyramid.
- ○ rectangular prism.

9. Which things have a line of symmetry?

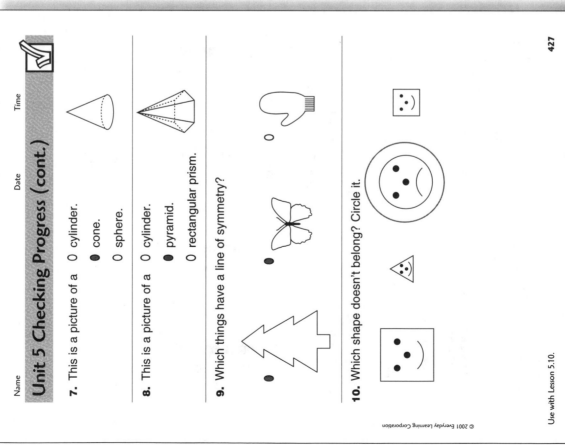

10. Which shape doesn't belong? Circle it.

Use with Lesson 5.10.

427

Name Date Time

Unit 7 Checking Progress

1. Solve.

23 + 7 = 30

9 + 51 = 60

40 = 8 + 32

70 = 66 + 4

2. Solve.

47 + 13 = 60

90 = 36 + 54

11 + 39 = 50

40 = 28 + 12

3. Find the median.

7, 3, 4 4

27, 45, 63, 45, 50 45

3, 9, 7, 14, 12 9

3, 5, 9, 7 5, 6, or 7

4. Add.

15 + 13 + 17 = 45

50 = 15 + 25 + 10

75 = 26 + 24 + 25

22 + 18 + 15 + 14 = 69

5. Measure each line to the nearest inch.

about 5 inches

about 3 inches

Name Date Time

Unit 7 Checking Progress (cont.)

6. Measure each line to the nearest centimeter.

about 8 centimeters

about 13 cm

7. Solve the number-grid puzzles.

43	44	45
53		
63		

		438
446	447	
456	457	
466		468
476		
486		

231	232	233	234
241	242		244
251			
261	262	263	
271		273	
281			

Unit 9 Checking Progress

Name _____ Date _____ Time _____

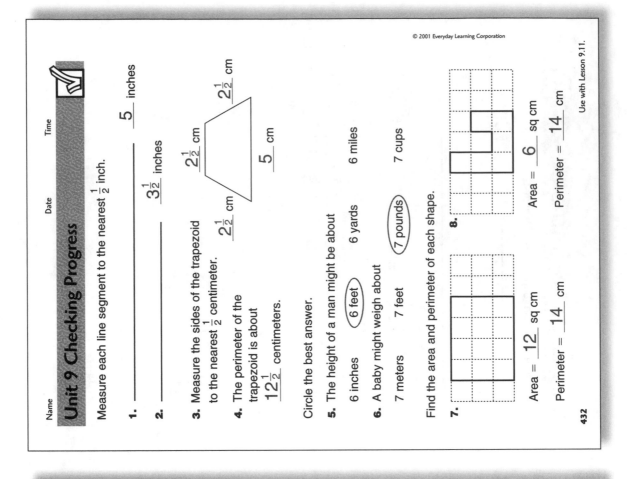

Measure each line segment to the nearest $\frac{1}{2}$ inch.

1. _____ __5__ inches

2. _____ $3\frac{1}{2}$ inches

3. Measure the sides of the trapezoid to the nearest $\frac{1}{2}$ centimeter.

$2\frac{1}{2}$ cm $2\frac{1}{2}$ cm

$2\frac{1}{2}$ cm   __5__ cm

4. The perimeter of the trapezoid is about $12\frac{1}{2}$ centimeters.

Circle the best answer.

5. The height of a man might be about

6 inches   (6 feet)   6 yards   6 miles

6. A baby might weigh about

7 meters   7 feet   (7 pounds)   7 cups

Find the area and perimeter of each shape.

7.

Area = __12__ sq cm

Perimeter = __14__ cm

8.

Area = __6__ sq cm

Perimeter = __14__ cm

Use with Lesson 9.11.

Unit 8 Checking Progress

Name _____ Date _____ Time _____

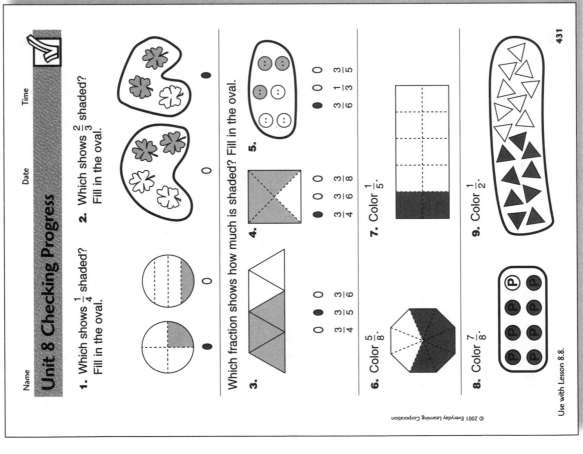

1. Which shows $\frac{1}{4}$ shaded? Fill in the oval.

○   ○   ●

2. Which shows $\frac{2}{3}$ shaded? Fill in the oval.

●   ○

Which fraction shows how much is shaded? Fill in the oval.

3.

○   ●
$\frac{3}{4}$ $\frac{3}{5}$

4.

○   ●   ○
$\frac{3}{4}$ $\frac{3}{6}$ $\frac{3}{8}$

5.

○   ○   ●
$\frac{3}{6}$ $\frac{1}{3}$ $\frac{3}{5}$

6. Color $\frac{5}{8}$.

7. Color $\frac{1}{5}$.

8. Color $\frac{7}{8}$.

9. Color $\frac{1}{2}$.

Use with Lesson 8.8.

Name _____ Date _____ Time _____

Unit 10 Checking Progress

1. Write the amount.

$1 Q Q Q D D D N P P P = $ __1.89__

2. Use $1 , Q , D , N , and P . Show $1.83 in two different ways.

Sample answers: $1 Q Q Q N P P P or

Q Q Q Q Q N N N N P P P

Complete.

3. 1 quarter = __5__ nickels

4. 1 dollar = __10__ dimes

5. 1 dime = __10__ pennies

6. 1 dollar = __100__ pennies

7. 1 dime = __2__ nickels

8. You buy:

Oranges
1 lb at $1.49 lb

and Yogurt
6-pack at $2.09

a. Estimate the total cost.

Estimated cost: $ __1.50__ + $ __2.10__ = $ __3.60__

b. Find the exact cost, with or without a calculator.

Exact cost: $ __3.58__

Use with Lesson 10.12.

433

Name _____ Date _____ Time _____

Unit 10 Checking Progress (cont.)

9. You have $5.00. You buy:

Cheese
8 oz. for $1.49

and Bananas
1 lb at 59¢ lb

and Bread
16 oz for 99¢

a. Estimate the total cost.

Estimated cost: $ __1.50__ + $ __0.60__ + $ __1.00__ = $ __3.10__

b. Find the exact cost, with or without a calculator.

Exact cost: $ __3.07__

c. Find the amount of change you will get back from $5.00. You may use your calculator.

Change: $ __1.93__

Fill in the blanks. Write ones, tens, hundreds, thousands, or ten-thousands.

10. The 7 in 3,745 stands for 7 __hundreds__ .

11. The 3 in 36,051 stands for 3 __ten-thousands__ .

12. The 6 in 465 stands for 6 __tens__ .

13. The 8 in 21,938 stands for 8 __ones__ .

14. The 2 in 92,645 stands for 2 __thousands__ .

Use with Lesson 10.12.

434

Name _____ Date _____ Time _____

Unit 12 Checking Progress

Record the time shown on the clock.

1.  3 : 55

2.  6 : 25

3. 9 : 40

Draw the hour and minute hands to match the time.

4. 4:10

5. 10:50

6. 2:05

7. Write the fact family for the Fact Triangle.

42
7   6
×, ÷

6 × 7 = 42   42 ÷ 7 = 6

7 × 6 = 42   42 ÷ 6 = 7

Solve.

8. 6 × 10 = 60

9. 2 × 7 = 14

10. 6 = 3 × 2

11. 20 = 4 × 5

12. 30 = 3 × 10

13. 3 × 5 = 15

14. 6 × 2 = 12

15. 5 × 6 = 30

16. 70 = 7 × 10

Use with Lesson 12.8.

Name _____ Date _____ Time _____

Unit 11 Checking Progress

Add or subtract.

1. $1.30
   − $0.64 | Answer | $0.66 |

2. $3.46
   + $1.78 | Answer | $5.24 |

3. $5.82
   − $2.47 | Answer | $3.35 |

Multiply. If you need help, make arrays with 0s or Xs.

4. 3 × 6 = 18

5. 5 × 4 = 20

6. 8 × 3 = 24

7. Write the fact family for the Fact Triangle.

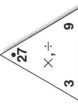

27
3   9
×, ÷

3 × 9 = 27

9 × 3 = 27

27 ÷ 3 = 9

27 ÷ 9 = 3

8. Write a multiplication story and a division story on the back of this page. **Answers vary.**

• Draw a picture or diagram.

• Write the answer.

• Write a number model.

Use with Lesson 11.10.

Name   Date   Time

Midyear Assessment

1. Find the rule and complete the table.

Rule	in	out
Subtract $0.25	$1.25	$1.00
	$0.30	$0.05
	$1.00	$0.75
	$2.40	$2.15
	Answers vary.	

2. Complete the Fact Triangle. Write the fact family.

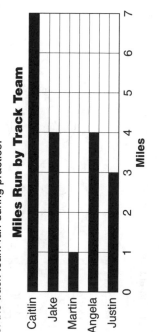

$5 + 7 = 12$

$7 + 5 = 12$

$12 - 5 = 7$

$12 - 7 = 5$

3. 524

Which digit is in the tens place? __2__

Which digit is in the hundreds place? __5__

Which digit is in the ones place? __4__

What is the smallest number
you can make with these 3 digits? __245__

438

Use with Lesson 6.12.

Name   Date   Time

Unit 12 Checking Progress (cont.)

The bar graph below shows the number of miles each member
of the track team ran during practice.

Miles Run by Track Team

Caitlin, Jake, Martin, Angela, Justin

Miles (0–7)

17. What was the fewest number of miles? __1__ mile

What was the greatest number of miles? __7__ miles

18. What is the difference between the fewest
and the greatest numbers of miles (range)? __6__ miles

19. What is the middle number of miles (median)? __4__ miles

20. Who ran fewer miles than Justin? __Martin__

Who ran more miles than Angela? __Caitlin__

21. What is the number of miles that occurred most often (mode)?

__4__ miles

437

Use with Lesson 12.8.

Midyear Assessment (cont.)

Name   Date   Time

4. Write at least 5 names in the 100-box.

100	Sample answers:
	25 + 25 + 25;
	40 + 60; *ciento*;
	300 − 200;
	90 + 30 − 20

5. What is the total value of the coins?

Ⓠ Ⓠ Ⓓ Ⓓ Ⓓ Ⓓ
Ⓝ Ⓝ Ⓟ

$ __1.11__

6. Carlos had 40 cents. His brother gave him 70 cents.

How much money does Carlos have now? __$1.10__, or 110¢

7. Jenna has 60 dolls in her collection. Tyshona has 20 dolls.

How many more dolls does Jenna have? __40__ more dolls

Is the answer to the question an odd or even number? __even__

8. Fill in the frames.

15 → 17 → 19 → 21

38 → 36 → 31 → 26

| **Rule** |
| +2 |

| **Rule** |
| +5 |

439

Midyear Assessment (cont.)

Name   Date   Time

Solve.

9.

34
+ 21
___
55

49
+ 18
___
67

10.

65
− 43
___
22

42
− 26
___
16

11. This shape is a

● hexagon
0 rhombus
0 trapezoid

12. This is a picture of a

0 pyramid
● cylinder
0 rectangular prism

13. Draw the hour and minute hands to show 6:40.

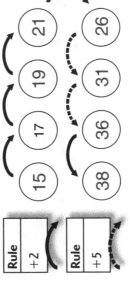

How many minutes until 7:00? __20__ minutes

440

Name   Date   Time

End-of-Year Assessment

1. Measure the line segment to the nearest inch and to the nearest centimeter.

_4_ inches   _11_ centimeters

2. Circle the correct unit of measure.

Allison weighs 50

(pounds)   miles   gallons

Jake ran 6

inches   feet   (miles)

Kenneth filled the car's tank with 10 _____ of gasoline.

cups   (gallons)   quarts

3. The temperature is _46_ °F.

°F
—50
—40

Use with Lesson 12.8.

441

Name   Date   Time

End-of-Year Assessment (cont.)

4. Complete the bar graph.

Tia read 6 books.
Ian read 3 books.
Theo read 5 books.

Number of Books Read

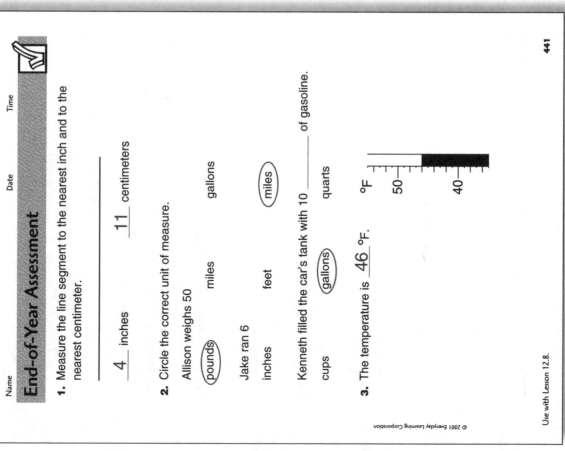

Books

7
6
5
4
3
2
1
0
    Tia   Ian   Theo

Maximum number of books: _6_

Minimum number of books: _3_

Median number of books: _5_

5. If [hexagon] is the ONE, then [triangle] is _1/6_ .

6. What fraction of the circles is shaded? _4/10 or 2/5_

Use with Lesson 12.8.

442

Name _____ Date _____ Time _____

End-of-Year Assessment (cont.)

7. Color $\frac{1}{4}$.

Fill in the oval next to the best estimate.

8. 138 + 263 is about _____
- 0 200
- 0 300
- ● 400

9. 92 − 59 is about _____
- 0 20
- ● 30
- 0 40

10. The perimeter of the rectangle is
16 centimeters.

The area of the rectangle is
15 square centimeters.

11.
```
  56      124
+ 67    + 208
─────    ─────
 123      332
```

12.
```
  72      346
- 46    - 183
─────    ─────
  26      163
```

Use with Lesson 12.8.

443

Name _____ Date _____ Time _____

End-of-Year Assessment (cont.)

13. This shape is a ...
- 0 hexagon
- 0 rhombus
- ● trapezoid

14. This shape is a ...
- ● pyramid
- 0 cylinder
- 0 rectangular prism

15. Complete the number grid.

742	743	744
752		754
762		
	773	

Write the time.

16. 3 : 45

17. 8 : 05

18. 11 : 31

Use with Lesson 12.8.

444

Name _____ Date _____ Time _____

End-of-Year Assessment (cont.)

22. 15 stickers. 3 children.

How many stickers per child? __5__ stickers

40 candies. 4 candies per child.

How many children? __10__ children

23. Find the rule and complete the table.

Rule
Multiply by 2

in	out
3	6
5	10
7	14
9	18
Answers vary.	

24. Complete.

1 week = __7__ days

1 day = __24__ hours

1 hour = __60__ minutes

1 minute = __60__ seconds

Use with Lesson 12.8.

Name _____ Date _____ Time _____

End-of-Year Assessment (cont.)

19. In the number 3,761 …

Which digit is in the tens place? __6__

Which digit is in the hundreds place? __7__

Which digit is in the ones place? __1__

Which digit is in the thousands place? __3__

What is the smallest number
you can make with these 4 digits? __1,367__

20. Insert <, >, or =.

209 __<__ 2,009

462 __<__ 624

5,421 __=__ 5,421

7,036 __>__ 6,704

21. 4 rows of chairs. 5 chairs in each row.

How many chairs in all? __20__ chairs

3 boxes of cookies. 10 cookies per box.

How many cookies in all? __30__ cookies

Use with Lesson 12.8.

End-of-Year Assessment (cont.)

Name _____ Date _____ Time _____

25. Ian saved $4.35 for his mother's birthday present.
His sister saved $3.90.
How much money did they save altogether?
Write a number model.

Answer: __$8.25__

Number model: ___$4.35 + $3.90 = $8.25___

26. Caitlin had $9.50 in her wallet.
She spent $6.75 at the movies.
How much money does she have now?
Write a number model.

Answer: __$2.75__

Number model: ___$9.50 − $6.75 = $2.75___

447

Class Checklist: Unit 1

Class _____

Dates _____

Learning Goals

1a Calculate the values of coin and bill combinations.
1b Know addition facts for sums to 10.
1c Identify place value for ones, tens, and hundreds.
1d Complete number sequences; identify and use number patterns to solve problems.
1e Find equivalent names for numbers.
1f Compare numbers; write the symbol <, >, or =.
1g Count by 2s, 5s, and 10s.
1h Make tallies and give the total.

Children's Names

1.
2.
3.
4.
5.
6.
7.
8.
9.
10.
11.
12.
13.
14.
15.
16.
17.
18.
19.
20.
21.
22.
23.
24.
25.
26.
27.
28.
29.
30.

448

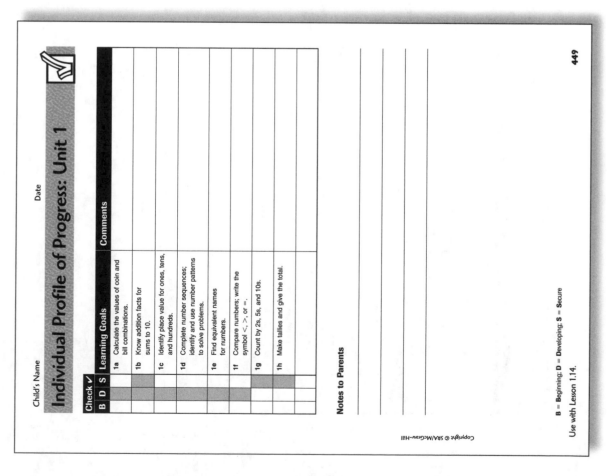

Class Checklist: Unit 2

Class _____

Dates _____

Learning Goals

- 2a Know "harder" subtraction facts.
- 2b Know "harder" addition facts.
- 2c Know "easier" subtraction facts.
- 2d Complete "What's My Rule?" tables.
- 2e Solve subtraction number stories.
- 2f Know "easier" addition facts.
- 2g Know "easier" addition facts.
- 2h Construct fact families for addition and subtraction.
- 2h Complete Frames-and-Arrows diagrams.
- 2i Solve addition number stories.
- 2j Find equivalent names for numbers.

Children's Names

1.
2.
3.
4.
5.
6.
7.
8.
9.
10.
11.
12.
13.
14.
15.
16.
17.
18.
19.
20.
21.
22.
23.
24.
25.
26.
27.
28.
29.
30.

450

Use with Lesson 2.14.

Child's Name _____   Date _____

Individual Profile of Progress: Unit 1

Check ✔			Learning Goals	Comments
B	D	S		
			1a Calculate the values of coin and bill combinations.	
			1b Know addition facts for sums to 10.	
			1c Identify place value for ones, tens, and hundreds.	
			1d Complete number sequences; identify and use number patterns to solve problems.	
			1e Find equivalent names for numbers.	
			1f Compare numbers; write the symbol <, >, or =.	
			1g Count by 2s, 5s, and 10s.	
			1h Make tallies and give the total.	

Notes to Parents

B = Beginning; D = Developing; S = Secure

Use with Lesson 1.14.

449

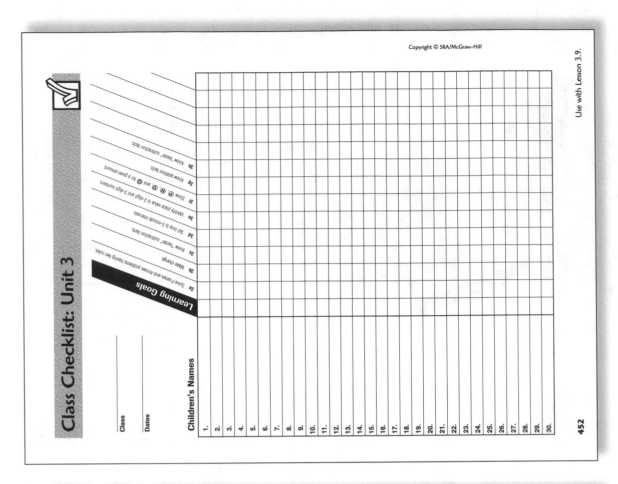

Class Checklist: Unit 3

Class _____

Dates _____

Learning Goals

3a Solve Frames-and-Arrows problems having two rules.
3b Make change.
3c Know "harder" subtraction facts.
3d Tell time to 5-minute intervals.
3e Identify place value in 2-digit and 3-digit numbers.
3f Show ⓣ, ⓝ, ⓓ, and ⓠ for a given amount.
3g Know addition facts.
3h Know "easier" subtraction facts.

Children's Names

1.
2.
3.
4.
5.
6.
7.
8.
9.
10.
11.
12.
13.
14.
15.
16.
17.
18.
19.
20.
21.
22.
23.
24.
25.
26.
27.
28.
29.
30.

Use with Lesson 3.9.

452

Child's Name _____ Date _____

Individual Profile of Progress: Unit 2

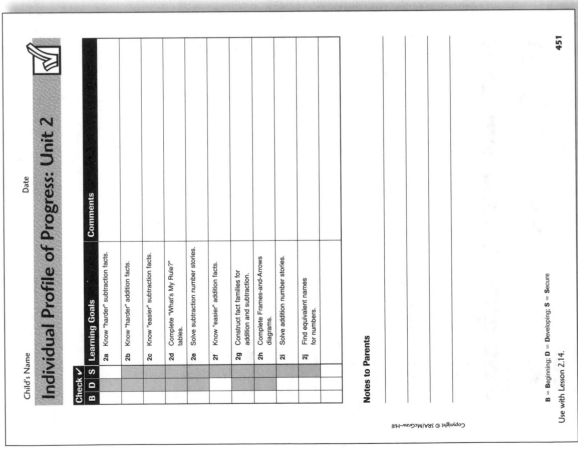

Check ✔			Learning Goals	Comments
B	D	S		
			2a Know "harder" subtraction facts.	
			2b Know "harder" addition facts.	
			2c Know "easier" subtraction facts.	
			2d Complete "What's My Rule?" tables.	
			2e Solve subtraction number stories.	
			2f Know "easier" addition facts.	
			2g Construct fact families for addition and subtraction.	
			2h Complete Frames-and-Arrows diagrams.	
			2i Solve addition number stories.	
			2j Find equivalent names for numbers.	

Notes to Parents

_____

_____

_____

B = Beginning; **D** = Developing; **S** = Secure

Use with Lesson 2.14.

451

Class Checklist: Unit 4

Class _____

Dates _____

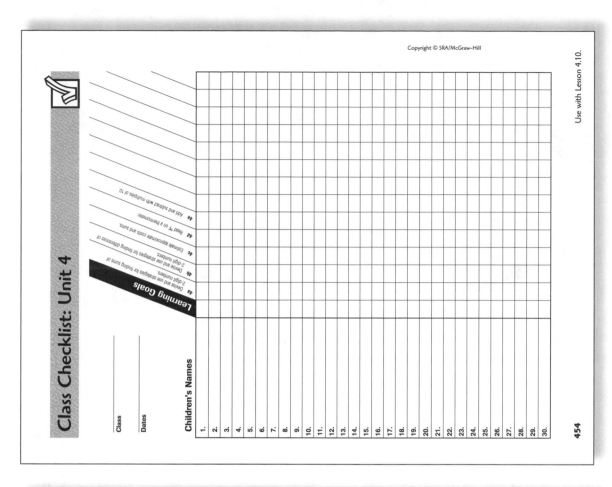

Learning Goals

4a Devise and use strategies for finding sums of 2-digit numbers.
4b Devise and use strategies for finding differences of 2-digit numbers.
4c Estimate approximate costs and sums.
4d Read °F on a thermometer.
4e Add and subtract with multiples of 10.

Children's Names

1.
2.
3.
4.
5.
6.
7.
8.
9.
10.
11.
12.
13.
14.
15.
16.
17.
18.
19.
20.
21.
22.
23.
24.
25.
26.
27.
28.
29.
30.

454

Use with Lesson 4.10.

Child's Name _____ Date _____

Individual Profile of Progress: Unit 3

Check ✔			Learning Goals	Comments
B	D	S		
			3a Solve Frames-and-Arrows problems having two rules.	
			3b Make change.	
			3c Know "harder" subtraction facts.	
			3d Tell time to 5-minute intervals.	
			3e Identify place value in 2-digit and 3-digit numbers.	
			3f Show Ⓟ, Ⓝ, Ⓓ, and @ for a given amount.	
			3g Know addition facts.	
			3h Know "easier" subtraction facts.	

Notes to Parents

B = Beginning; D = Developing; S = Secure

Use with Lesson 3.9.

453

Class Checklist: Unit 5

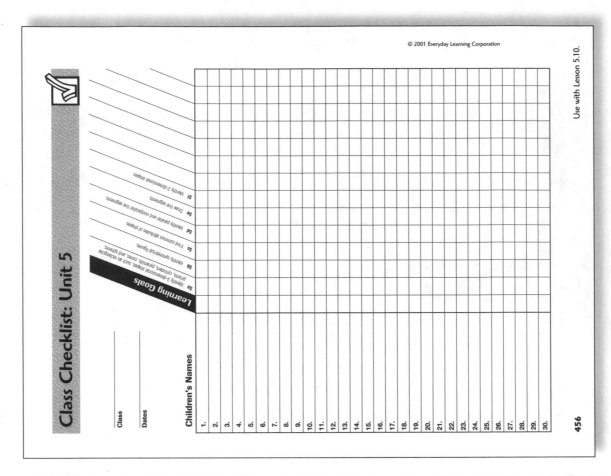

Class

Dates

Learning Goals

5a Identify 3-dimensional shapes, such as rectangular prisms, cylinders, pyramids, cones, and spheres.

5b Identify symmetrical figures.

5c Find common attributes of shapes.

5d Identify parallel and nonparallel line segments.

5e Draw line segments.

5f Identify 2-dimensional shapes.

Children's Names

1.
2.
3.
4.
5.
6.
7.
8.
9.
10.
11.
12.
13.
14.
15.
16.
17.
18.
19.
20.
21.
22.
23.
24.
25.
26.
27.
28.
29.
30.

Use with Lesson 5.10.

456

Child's Name _____ Date _____

Individual Profile of Progress: Unit 4

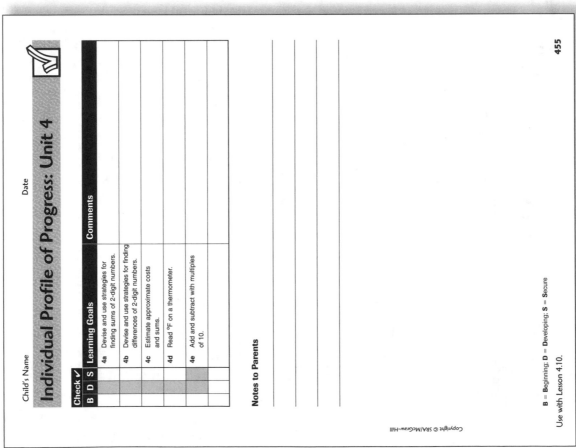

Check ✓

B	D	S	Learning Goals	Comments
			4a Devise and use strategies for finding sums of 2-digit numbers.	
			4b Devise and use strategies for finding differences of 2-digit numbers.	
			4c Estimate approximate costs and sums.	
			4d Read °F on a thermometer.	
			4e Add and subtract with multiples of 10.	

Notes to Parents

B = Beginning; **D** = Developing; **S** = Secure

Use with Lesson 4.10.

455

Class Checklist: Unit 6

Class _____

Dates _____

Learning Goals

- **6a** Solve stories about multiples of equal groups.
- **6b** Solve equal-grouping and equal-sharing division problems.
- **6c** Use the trade-first method to solve 2-digit subtraction problems.
- **6d** Make ballpark estimates of exact answers.
- **6e** Model multiplication problems with arrays.
- **6f** Add three 2-digit numbers mentally.
- **6g** Add and subtract with multiples of 10.
- **6h** Solve addition and subtraction number stories.
- **6i** Add three 1-digit numbers mentally.

Children's Names

1.
2.
3.
4.
5.
6.
7.
8.
9.
10.
11.
12.
13.
14.
15.
16.
17.
18.
19.
20.
21.
22.
23.
24.
25.
26.
27.
28.
29.
30.

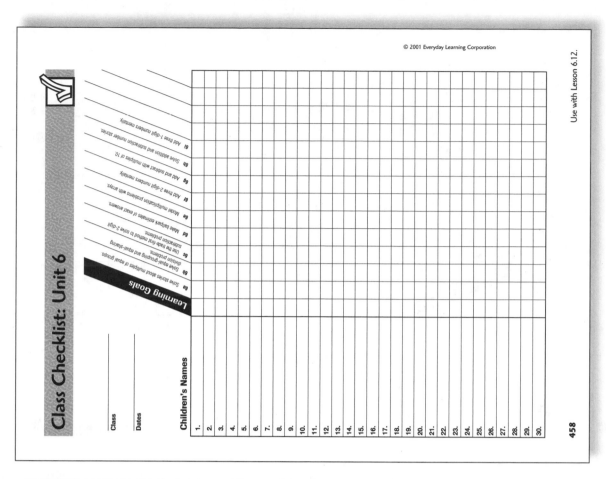

Use with Lesson 6.12.

458

Child's Name _____   Date _____

Individual Profile of Progress: Unit 5

Check ✓			Learning Goals	Comments
B	D	S		
			5a Identify 3-dimensional shapes, such as rectangular prisms, cylinders, pyramids, cones, and spheres.	
			5b Identify symmetrical figures.	
			5c Find common attributes of shapes.	
			5d Identify parallel and nonparallel line segments.	
			5e Draw line segments.	
			5f Identify 2-dimensional shapes.	

Notes to Parents

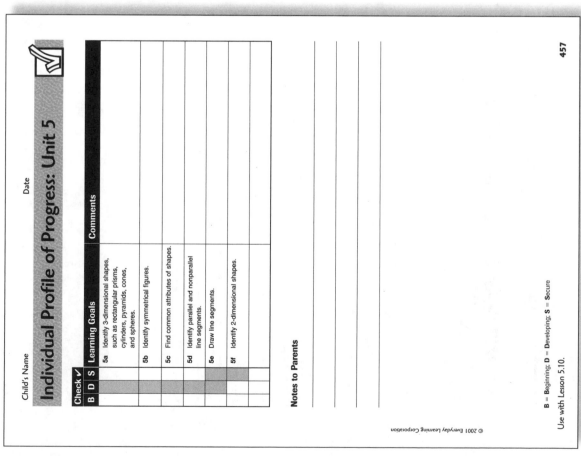

B = Beginning; **D** = Developing; **S** = Secure

Use with Lesson 5.10.

457

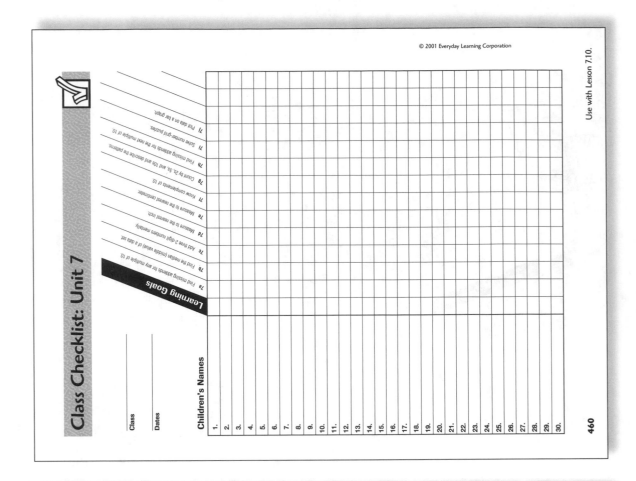

Class Checklist: Unit 7

Class _____

Dates _____

Learning Goals

7a Find missing addends for any multiple of 10.
7b Find the median (middle value) of a data set.
7c Add three 2-digit numbers mentally.
7d Measure to the nearest inch.
7e Measure to the nearest centimeter.
7f Know complements of 10.
7g Count by 2s, 5s, and 10s and describe the patterns.
7h Find missing addends for the next multiple of 10.
7i Solve number-grid puzzles.
7j Plot data on a bar graph.

Children's Names

1.
2.
3.
4.
5.
6.
7.
8.
9.
10.
11.
12.
13.
14.
15.
16.
17.
18.
19.
20.
21.
22.
23.
24.
25.
26.
27.
28.
29.
30.

Use with Lesson 7.10.

460

Child's Name _____ Date _____

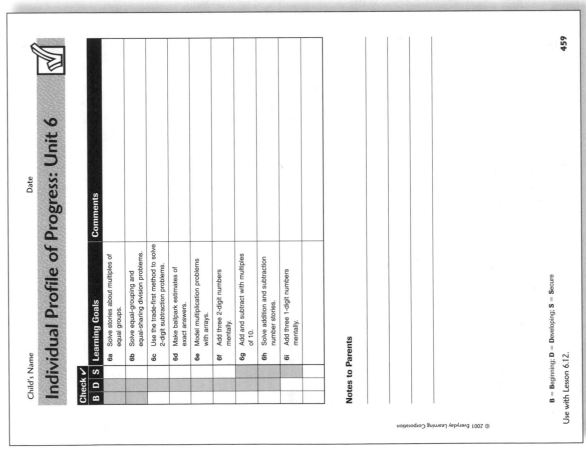

Individual Profile of Progress: Unit 6

Check ✔			Learning Goals	Comments
B	D	S		
			6a Solve stories about multiples of equal groups.	
			6b Solve equal-grouping and equal-sharing division problems.	
			6c Use the trade-first method to solve 2-digit subtraction problems.	
			6d Make ballpark estimates of exact answers.	
			6e Model multiplication problems with arrays.	
			6f Add three 2-digit numbers mentally.	
			6g Add and subtract with multiples of 10.	
			6h Solve addition and subtraction number stories.	
			6i Add three 1-digit numbers mentally.	

Notes to Parents _____

459

B = Beginning; **D** = Developing; **S** = Secure

Use with Lesson 6.12.

Class Checklist: Unit 8

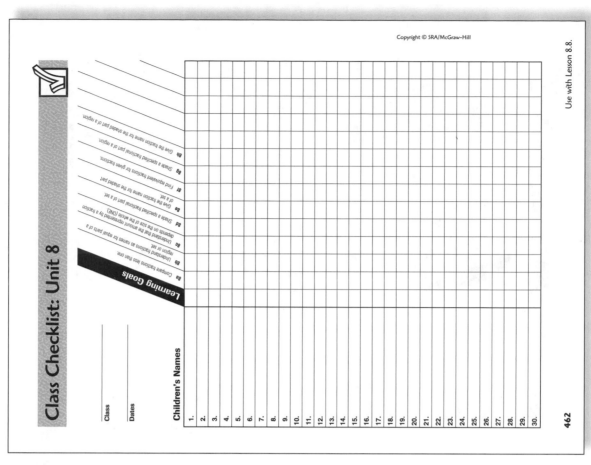

Class _____

Dates _____

Learning Goals

8a Compare fractions less than one.
8b Understand fractions as names for equal parts of a region or set.
8c Understand that the amount represented by a fraction depends on the size of the whole (ONE).
8d Shade a specified fractional part of a set.
8e Give the fraction name for the shaded part of a set.
8f Find equivalent fractions for given fractions.
8g Shade a specified fractional part of a region.
8h Give the fraction name for the shaded part of a region.

Children's Names

1.
2.
3.
4.
5.
6.
7.
8.
9.
10.
11.
12.
13.
14.
15.
16.
17.
18.
19.
20.
21.
22.
23.
24.
25.
26.
27.
28.
29.
30.

Use with Lesson 8.8.

462

Child's Name _____   Date _____

Individual Profile of Progress: Unit 7

Check ✓			Learning Goals	Comments
B	**D**	**S**		
			7a Find missing addends for any multiple of 10.	
			7b Find the median (middle value) of a data set.	
			7c Add three 2-digit numbers mentally.	
			7d Measure to the nearest inch.	
			7e Measure to the nearest centimeter.	
			7f Know complements of 10.	
			7g Count by 2s, 5s, and 10s and describe the patterns.	
			7h Find missing addends for the next multiple of 10.	
			7i Solve number-grid puzzles.	
			7j Plot data on a bar graph.	

Notes to Parents

B = Beginning; **D** = Developing; **S** = Secure

Use with Lesson 7.10.

461

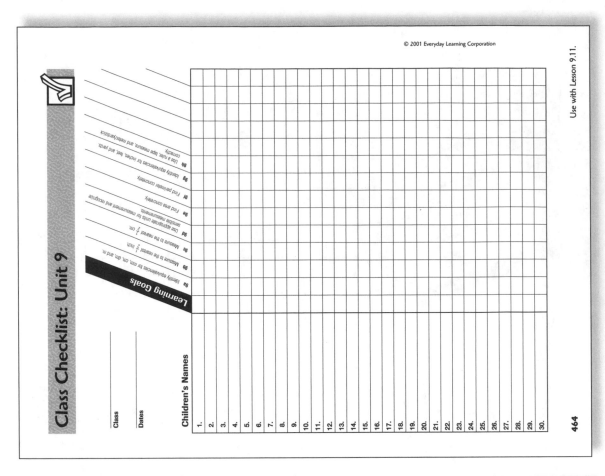

Class Checklist: Unit 9

Class _____

Dates _____

Learning Goals	9a Identify equivalences for mm, cm, dm, and m.	9b Measure to the nearest ½ inch.	9c Measure to the nearest ½ cm.	9d Use appropriate units for measurement and recognize sensible measurements.	9e Find area concretely.	9f Find perimeter correctly.	9g Identify equivalencies for inches, feet, and yards.	9h Use a ruler, tape measure, and meter/yardstick correctly.			

Children's Names

1.
2.
3.
4.
5.
6.
7.
8.
9.
10.
11.
12.
13.
14.
15.
16.
17.
18.
19.
20.
21.
22.
23.
24.
25.
26.
27.
28.
29.
30.

464

Use with Lesson 9.11.

Child's Name _____ Date _____

Individual Profile of Progress: Unit 8

Check ✓			Learning Goals	Comments
B	D	S		
			8a Compare fractions less than one.	
			8b Understand fractions as names for equal parts of a region or set.	
			8c Understand that the amount represented by a fraction depends on the size of the whole (ONE).	
			8d Shade a specified fractional part of a set.	
			8e Give the fraction name for the shaded part of a set.	
			8f Find equivalent fractions for given fractions.	
			8g Shade a specified fractional part of a region.	
			8h Give the fraction name for the shaded part of a region.	

Notes to Parents

_____

_____

_____

B = Beginning; **D** = Developing; **S** = Secure

Use with Lesson 8.8.

463

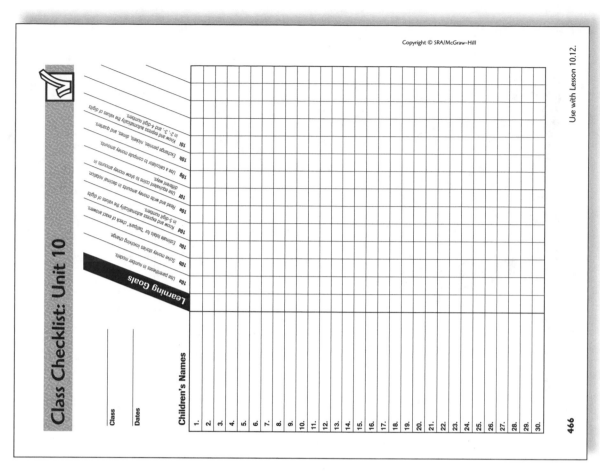

Class Checklist: Unit 10

Class _____

Dates _____

Learning Goals

	Use parentheses in number models.	10a
10b	Solve money stories involving change.	10c
Estimate totals for "ballpark" check of exact answers.	10d	Know and express automatically the values of digits in 5-digit numbers.
Read and write money amounts in decimal notation.	10e	Use equivalent coins to show money amounts in different ways.
10f	Use a calculator to compute money amounts.	10g
Exchange pennies, nickels, dimes, and quarters.	10h	Know and express automatically the values of digits in 2-, 3-, and 4-digit numbers.

Children's Names

1.
2.
3.
4.
5.
6.
7.
8.
9.
10.
11.
12.
13.
14.
15.
16.
17.
18.
19.
20.
21.
22.
23.
24.
25.
26.
27.
28.
29.
30.

Use with Lesson 10.12.

466

Child's Name _____ Date _____

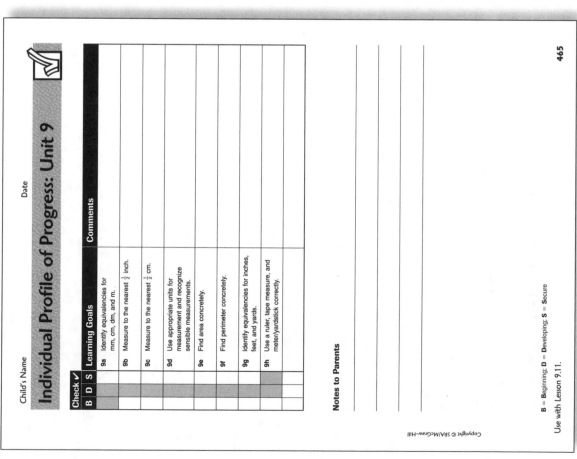

Individual Profile of Progress: Unit 9

Check ✔			Learning Goals	Comments
B	**D**	**S**		
			9a Identify equivalencies for mm, cm, dm, and m.	
			9b Measure to the nearest $\frac{1}{2}$ inch.	
			9c Measure to the nearest $\frac{1}{2}$ cm.	
			9d Use appropriate units for measurement and recognize sensible measurements.	
			9e Find area concretely.	
			9f Find perimeter concretely.	
			9g Identify equivalencies for inches, feet, and yards.	
			9h Use a ruler, tape measure, and meter/yardstick correctly.	

Notes to Parents

_____

_____

_____

_____

B = Beginning; **D** = Developing; **S** = Secure

Use with Lesson 9.11.

465

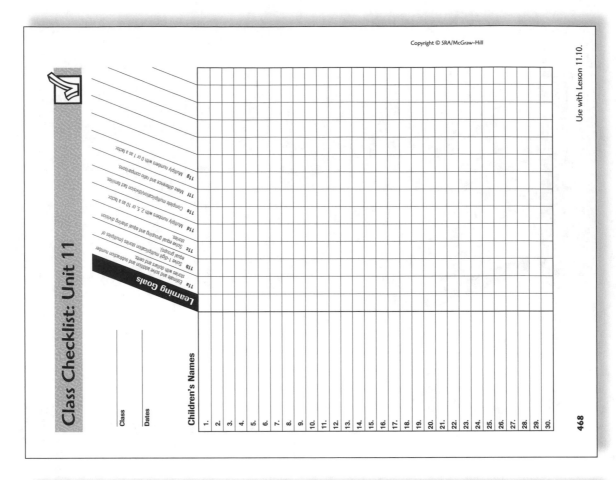

Class Checklist: Unit 11

Class _____

Dates _____

Learning Goals

11a Estimate and solve addition and subtraction number stories with dollars and cents.

11b Solve 1-digit multiplication stories involving equal groups.

11c Solve equal grouping and equal sharing division stories.

11d Multiply numbers with 2, 5, or 10 as a factor.

11e Complete multiplication/division fact families.

11f Make difference and ratio comparisons.

11g Multiply numbers with 0 or 1 as a factor.

Children's Names

1.
2.
3.
4.
5.
6.
7.
8.
9.
10.
11.
12.
13.
14.
15.
16.
17.
18.
19.
20.
21.
22.
23.
24.
25.
26.
27.
28.
29.
30.

Use with Lesson 11.10.

468

Child's Name _____ Date _____

Individual Profile of Progress: Unit 10

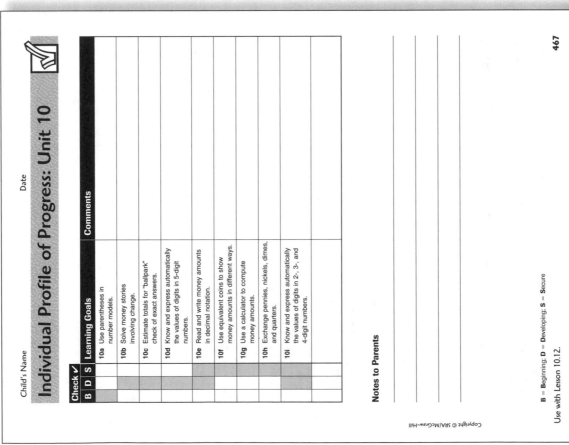

Check ✔			Learning Goals	Comments
B	D	S		
			10a Use parentheses in number models.	
			10b Solve money stories involving change.	
			10c Estimate totals for "ballpark" check of exact answers.	
			10d Know and express automatically the values of digits in 5-digit numbers.	
			10e Read and write money amounts in decimal notation.	
			10f Use equivalent coins to show money amounts in different ways.	
			10g Use a calculator to compute money amounts.	
			10h Exchange pennies, nickels, dimes, and quarters.	
			10i Know and express automatically the values of digits in 2-, 3-, and 4-digit numbers.	

Notes to Parents

_____

_____

_____

B = Beginning; D = Developing; S = Secure

Use with Lesson 10.12.

467

Class Checklist: Unit 12

Class

Dates

Learning Goals

12a Use alternate names for times.
12b Know multiplication facts.
12c Determine the mode of a data set.
12d Determine the median, maximum, minimum, and range of a data set.
12e Complete multiplication/division fact families.
12f Multiply numbers with 2, 5, and 10 as a factor.
12g Tell time to 5-minute intervals.
12h Demonstrate calendar concepts and skills.
12i Compare quantities from a bar graph.

Children's Names

1.
2.
3.
4.
5.
6.
7.
8.
9.
10.
11.
12.
13.
14.
15.
16.
17.
18.
19.
20.
21.
22.
23.
24.
25.
26.
27.
28.
29.
30.

Use with Lesson 12.8.

470

Child's Name _____ Date _____

Individual Profile of Progress: Unit 11

Check ✓

B	D	S	Learning Goals	Comments
			11a Estimate and solve addition and subtraction number stories with dollars and cents.	
			11b Solve 1-digit multiplication stories (multiples of equal groups).	
			11c Solve equal grouping and equal sharing division stories.	
			11d Multiply numbers with 2, 5, or 10 as a factor.	
			11e Complete multiplication/division fact families.	
			11f Make difference and ratio comparisons.	
			11g Multiply numbers with 0 or 1 as a factor.	

Notes to Parents

B = Beginning; D = Developing; S = Secure

Use with Lesson 11.10.

469

Class Checklist: 1st Quarter

Class _____

Dates _____

Learning Goals

1. Calculate the values of coin and bill combinations. (1a)
2. Show ⓝ, ⓝ, and ⓓ for a given amount. (3a)
3. Make change. (3b)
4. Complete number sequences; identify and use number patterns to solve problems. (1d)
5. Compare numbers; write the symbol <, >, or = (1f)
6. Count by 2s, 5s, and 10s. (1g)
7. Make tables and give the total. (1h)
8. Find equivalent names for numbers. (1e, 2)
9. Construct fact families for addition and subtraction. (2a)
10. Solve subtraction number stories. (2e)
11. Solve addition number stories. (2)

Children's Names

1.
2.
3.
4.
5.
6.
7.
8.
9.
10.
11.
12.
13.
14.
15.
16.
17.
18.
19.
20.
21.
22.
23.
24.
25.
26.
27.
28.
29.
30.

Use with Lesson 3.9.

472

Child's Name _____   Date _____

Individual Profile of Progress: Unit 12

Check ✔			Learning Goals	Comments
B	D	S		
			12a Use alternate names for times.	
			12b Know multiplication facts.	
			12c Determine the mode of a data set.	
			12d Determine the median, maximum, minimum, and range of a data set.	
			12e Complete multiplication/division fact families.	
			12f Multiply numbers with 2, 5, and 10 as a factor.	
			12g Tell time to 5-minute intervals.	
			12h Demonstrate calendar concepts and skills.	
			12i Compare quantities from a bar graph.	

Notes to Parents

_____

_____

_____

B = Beginning; **D** = Developing; **S** = Secure

Use with Lesson 12.8.

471

Individual Profile of Progress: 1st Quarter

Child's Name _____ Date _____

Check ✔			Learning Goals	Comments
B	D	S		
			1. Calculate the values of coin and bill combinations. (1a)	
			2. Show ℗, ℕ, ⅅ, and ℚ for a given amount. (3f)	
			3. Make change. (3b)	
			4. Complete number sequences; identify and use number patterns to solve problems. (1d)	
			5. Compare numbers; write the symbol <, >, or =. (1f)	
			6. Count by 2s, 5s, and 10s. (1g)	
			7. Make tallies and give the total. (1h)	
			8. Find equivalent names for numbers. (1e, 2i)	
			9. Construct fact families for addition and subtraction. (2g)	
			10. Solve subtraction number stories. (2e)	
			11. Solve addition number stories. (2i)	
			12. Know "harder" subtraction facts. (2a, 3c)	
			13. Identify place value in 2-digit and 3-digit numbers. (1c, 3e)	
			14. Know addition facts. (1b, 2b, 2f, 3g)	
			15. Know "easier" subtraction facts. (2c, 3h)	
			16. Complete "What's My Rule?" tables. (2d)	
			17. Complete Frames-and-Arrows diagrams. (2h)	
			18. Solve Frames-and-Arrows problems having two rules. (3a)	
			19. Tell time to 5-minute intervals. (3d)	

B = Beginning; D = Developing; S = Secure

474

Use with Lesson 3.9.

Class Checklist: 1st Quarter (cont.)

Class _____

Dates _____

Learning Goals

12. Know "harder" subtraction facts. (2a, 3c)
13. Identify place value in 2-digit and 3-digit numbers. (1c, 3e)
14. Know addition facts. (1b, 2b, 2f, 3g)
15. Know "easier" subtraction facts. (2c, 3h)
16. Complete "What's My Rule?" tables. (2d)
17. Complete Frames-and-Arrows diagrams. (2h)
18. Solve Frames-and-Arrows problems having two rules. (3a)
19. Tell time to 5-minute intervals. (3d)

Children's Names

1.
2.
3.
4.
5.
6.
7.
8.
9.
10.
11.
12.
13.
14.
15.
16.
17.
18.
19.
20.
21.
22.
23.
24.
25.
26.
27.
28.
29.
30.

473

Use with Lesson 3.9.

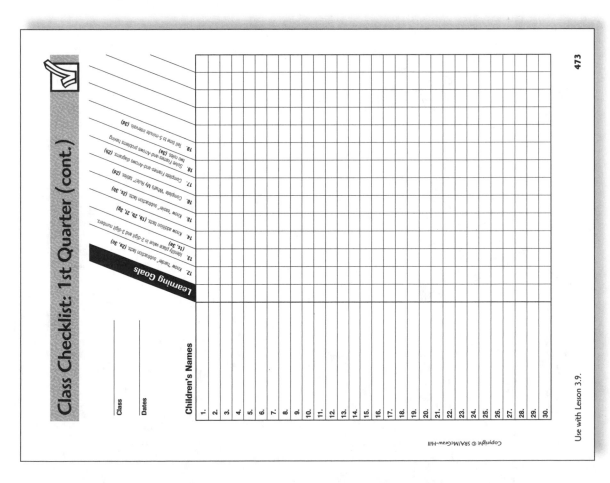

Class Checklist: 2nd Quarter (cont.)

Class _____

Dates _____

Learning Goals

13. Identify 3-dimensional shapes, such as rectangular prisms, cylinders, pyramids, cones, and spheres. (5a)
14. Identify symmetrical figures. (5b)
15. Find common attributes of shapes. (5c)
16. Identify parallel and nonparallel line segments. (5d)
17. Draw line segments. (5e)
18. Identify 2-dimensional shapes. (5f)
19. Read °F on a thermometer. (4d)

Children's Names

1. 2. 3. 4. 5. 6. 7. 8. 9. 10. 11. 12. 13. 14. 15. 16. 17. 18. 19. 20. 21. 22. 23. 24. 25. 26. 27. 28. 29. 30.

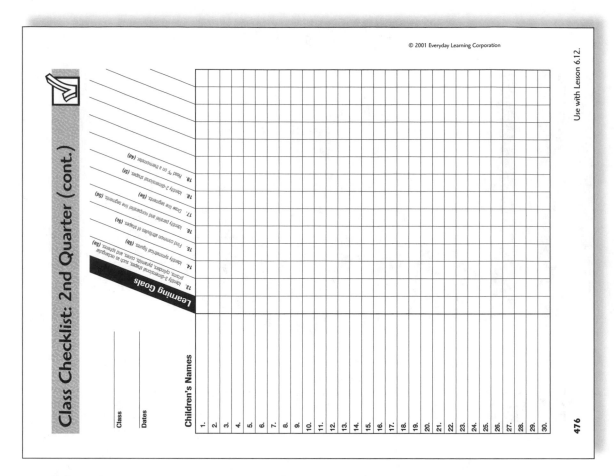

© 2001 Everyday Learning Corporation

Use with Lesson 6.12.

476

Class Checklist: 2nd Quarter

Class _____

Dates _____

Learning Goals

1. Devise and use strategies for finding sums of 2-digit numbers. (4a)
2. Devise and use strategies for finding differences of 2-digit numbers. (4b)
3. Estimate approximate costs and sums. (4c)
4. Solve stories about multiples of equal groups. (6g)
5. Use the trade-first method to solve 2-digit subtraction problems. (4c)
6. Make ballpark estimates of exact answers. (6d)
7. Add three 2-digit numbers mentally. (6a)
8. Add and subtract with multiples of 10. (4e, 6g)
9. Solve addition and subtraction number stories. (6h)
10. Add three 1-digit numbers mentally. (6a)
11. Solve equal-grouping and equal-sharing division problems. (6g)
12. Model multiplication problems with arrays. (6e)

Children's Names

1. 2. 3. 4. 5. 6. 7. 8. 9. 10. 11. 12. 13. 14. 15. 16. 17. 18. 19. 20. 21. 22. 23. 24. 25. 26. 27. 28. 29. 30.

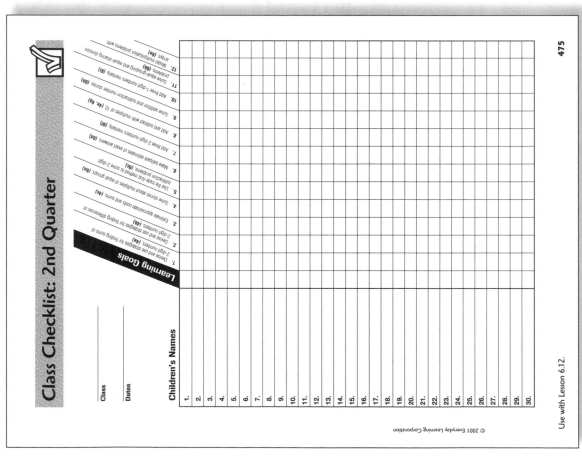

475

© 2001 Everyday Learning Corporation

Use with Lesson 6.12.

Class Checklist: 3rd Quarter

Class _____

Dates _____

Learning Goals

1. Find missing addends for any multiple of 10. (7a)
2. Add two 2-digit numbers mentally. (7a)
3. Know complements of 10. (7c)
4. Count by 2s, 5s, and 10s and describe the patterns. (7g)
5. Find missing addends for the next multiple of 10. (7i)
6. Solve number-grid puzzles. (7i)
7. Find the median (middle value) of a data set. (7b)
8. Plot data on a bar graph. (7j)
9. Measure to the nearest inch. (7d)
10. Measure to the nearest inch. (7d)
11. Identify the nearest centimeter. (7a)
12. Identify equivalencies for mm, cm, dm, and m. (9a)
13. Measure to the nearest $\frac{1}{2}$ inch. (9b)
13. Measure to the nearest $\frac{1}{2}$ cm. (9c)

Children's Names

1.
2.
3.
4.
5.
6.
7.
8.
9.
10.
11.
12.
13.
14.
15.
16.
17.
18.
19.
20.
21.
22.
23.
24.
25.
26.
27.
28.
29.
30.

478

Use with Lesson 9.11.

Child's Name _____   Date _____

Individual Profile of Progress: 2nd Quarter

Check ✔

B	D	S	Learning Goals	Comments
			1. Devise and use strategies for finding sums of 2-digit numbers. (4a)	
			2. Devise and use strategies for finding differences of 2-digit numbers. (4b)	
			3. Estimate approximate costs and sums. (4c)	
			4. Solve stories about multiples of equal groups. (6a)	
			5. Use the trade-first method to solve 2-digit subtraction problems. (6c)	
			6. Make ballpark estimates of exact answers. (6d)	
			7. Add three 2-digit numbers mentally. (6f)	
			8. Add and subtract with multiples of 10. (4e, 6g)	
			9. Solve addition and subtraction number stories. (6h)	
			10. Add three 1-digit numbers mentally. (6i)	
			11. Solve equal-grouping and equal-sharing division problems. (6b)	
			12. Model multiplication problems with arrays. (6e)	
			13. Identify 3-dimensional shapes, such as rectangular prisms, cylinders, pyramids, cones, and spheres. (5a)	
			14. Identify symmetrical figures. (5b)	
			15. Find common attributes of shapes. (5c)	
			16. Identify parallel and nonparallel line segments. (5d)	
			17. Draw line segments. (5e)	
			18. Identify 2-dimensional shapes. (5f)	
			19. Read °F on a thermometer. (4d)	

B = Beginning; D = Developing; S = Secure

Use with Lesson 6.12.

477

Child's Name _____ Date _____

Individual Profile of Progress: 3rd Quarter

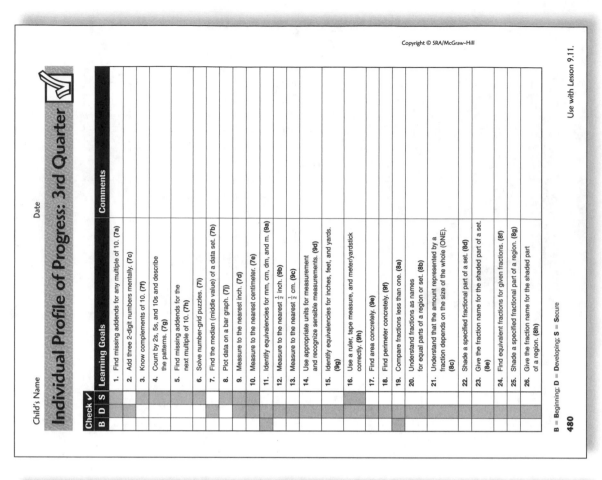

Check ✔			Learning Goals	Comments
B	**D**	**S**		
			1. Find missing addends for any multiple of 10. **(7a)**	
			2. Add three 2-digit numbers mentally. **(7c)**	
			3. Know complements of 10. **(7f)**	
			4. Count by 2s, 5s, and 10s and describe the patterns. **(7g)**	
			5. Find missing addends for the next multiple of 10. **(7h)**	
			6. Solve number-grid puzzles. **(7I)**	
			7. Find the median (middle value) of a data set. **(7b)**	
			8. Plot data on a bar graph. **(7I)**	
			9. Measure to the nearest inch. **(7d)**	
			10. Measure to the nearest centimeter. **(7e)**	
			11. Identify equivalencies for mm, cm, dm, and m. **(9a)**	
			12. Measure to the nearest $\frac{1}{2}$ inch. **(9b)**	
			13. Measure to the nearest $\frac{1}{2}$ cm. **(9c)**	
			14. Use appropriate units for measurement and recognize sensible measurements. **(9d)**	
			15. Identify equivalencies for inches, feet, and yards. **(9g)**	
			16. Use a ruler, tape measure, and meter/yardstick correctly. **(9h)**	
			17. Find area concretely. **(9e)**	
			18. Find perimeter concretely. **(9f)**	
			19. Compare fractions less than one. **(8a)**	
			20. Understand fractions as names for equal parts of a region or set. **(8b)**	
			21. Understand that the amount represented by a fraction depends on the size of the whole (ONE). **(8c)**	
			22. Shade a specified fractional part of a set. **(8d)**	
			23. Give the fraction name for the shaded part of a set. **(8e)**	
			24. Find equivalent fractions for given fractions. **(8f)**	
			25. Shade a specified fractional part of a region. **(8g)**	
			26. Give the fraction name for the shaded part of a region. **(8h)**	

B = Beginning; **D** = Developing; **S** = Secure

480

Use with Lesson 9.11.

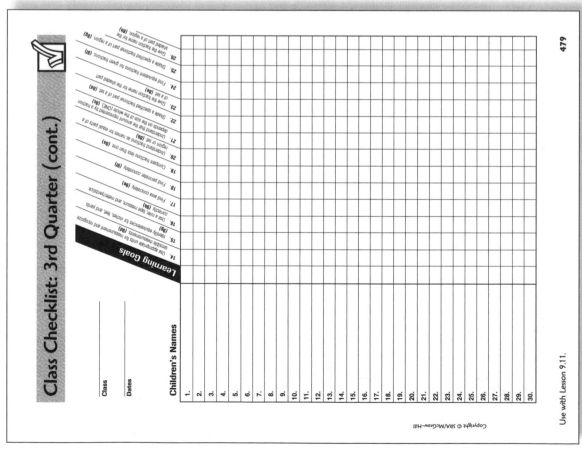

Class Checklist: 3rd Quarter (cont.)

Class _____

Dates _____

Learning Goals

14. Use appropriate units for measurement and recognize sensible measurements. **(9d)**
15. Identify equivalencies for inches, feet, and yards. **(9g)**
16. Use a ruler, tape measure, and meter/yardstick correctly. **(9h)**
17. Find area concretely. **(9e)**
18. Find perimeter concretely. **(9f)**
19. Compare fractions less than one. **(8a)**
20. Understand fractions as names for equal parts of a region or set. **(8b)**
21. Understand that the amount represented by a fraction depends on the size of the whole (ONE). **(8c)**
22. Shade a specified fractional part of a set. **(8d)**
23. Give the fraction name for the shaded part of a set. **(8e)**
24. Find equivalent fractions for given fractions. **(8f)**
25. Shade a specified fractional part of a region. **(8g)**
26. Give the fraction name for the shaded part of a region. **(8h)**

Children's Names

1.
2.
3.
4.
5.
6.
7.
8.
9.
10.
11.
12.
13.
14.
15.
16.
17.
18.
19.
20.
21.
22.
23.
24.
25.
26.
27.
28.
29.
30.

479

Use with Lesson 9.11.

Class Checklist: 4th Quarter (cont.)

Class _____
Dates _____

Learning Goals

12. Solve equal grouping and equal sharing division stories. (11a)
13. Make difference and ratio comparisons. (11)
14. Multiply numbers with 0 or 1 as a factor. (11g)
15. Know multiplication facts. (12b)
16. Complete multiplication/division fact families. (11e, 12a)
17. Multiply numbers with 2, 5, and 10 as a factor. (11d, 12f)
18. Use alternate names for times. (12a)
19. Tell time to 5-minute intervals. (12g)
20. Demonstrate calendar concepts and skills. (12h)
21. Determine the mode of a data set. (12c)
22. Determine the median, maximum, minimum, and range of a data set. (12d)
23. Compare quantities from a bar graph. (12i)

Children's Names

1.
2.
3.
4.
5.
6.
7.
8.
9.
10.
11.
12.
13.
14.
15.
16.
17.
18.
19.
20.
21.
22.
23.
24.
25.
26.
27.
28.
29.
30.

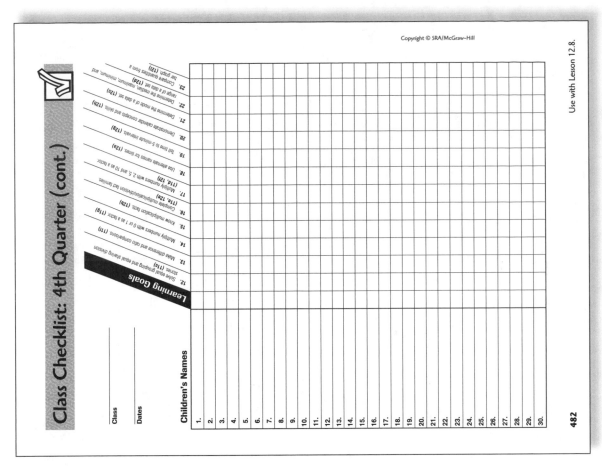

482

Use with Lesson 12.8.

Class Checklist: 4th Quarter

Class _____
Dates _____

Learning Goals

1. Use parentheses in number models. (10a)
2. Estimate totals for "ballpark" check of exact answers. (10c)
3. Know and express automatically the values of digits in 5-digit numbers. (10b)
4. Know and express automatically the values of digits in 2-, 3-, and 4-digit numbers. (10b)
5. Solve money stories involving change. (10e)
6. Read and write money amounts. (10d)
7. Use equivalent coins to show money amounts in different ways. (10f)
8. Use a calculator to compute money amounts. (10g)
9. Exchange pennies, nickels, dimes, and quarters. (10h)
10. Estimate and solve addition and subtraction number stories with dollars and cents. (11a)
11. Solve 1-digit multiplication stories (multiples of equal groups). (11b)

Children's Names

1.
2.
3.
4.
5.
6.
7.
8.
9.
10.
11.
12.
13.
14.
15.
16.
17.
18.
19.
20.
21.
22.
23.
24.
25.
26.
27.
28.
29.
30.

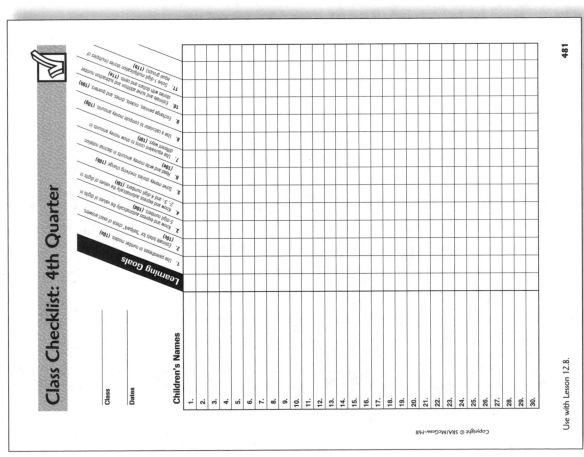

481

Use with Lesson 12.8.

List of Assessment Sources

Ongoing Assessment

Product Assessment

Periodic Assessment

Outside Tests

Other

Use as needed.

484

Child's Name _____   Date _____

Individual Profile of Progress: 4th Quarter

Check ✔			Learning Goals	Comments
B	D	S		
			1. Use parentheses in number models. (10a)	
			2. Estimate totals for "ballpark" check of exact answers. (10c)	
			3. Know and express automatically the values of digits in 5-digit numbers. (10d)	
			4. Know and express automatically the values of digits in 2-, 3-, and 4-digit numbers. (10i)	
			5. Solve money stories involving change. (10b)	
			6. Read and write money amounts in decimal notation. (10e)	
			7. Use equivalent coins to show money amounts in different ways. (10f)	
			8. Use a calculator to compute money amounts. (10g)	
			9. Exchange pennies, nickels, dimes, and quarters. (10h)	
			10. Estimate and solve addition and subtraction number stories with dollars and cents. (11a)	
			11. Solve 1-digit multiplication stories (multiples of equal groups). (11b)	
			12. Solve equal grouping and equal sharing division stories. (11c)	
			13. Make difference and ratio comparisons. (11f)	
			14. Multiply numbers with 0 or 1 as a factor. (11g)	
			15. Know multiplication facts. (12b)	
			16. Complete multiplication/division fact families. (11e, 12a)	
			17. Multiply numbers with 2, 5, and 10 as a factor. (11d, 12f)	
			18. Use alternate names for times. (12a)	
			19. Tell time to 5-minute intervals. (12g)	
			20. Demonstrate calendar concepts and skills. (12h)	
			21. Determine the mode of a data set. (12c)	
			22. Determine the median, maximum, minimum, and range of a data set. (12d)	
			23. Compare quantities from a bar graph. (12i)	

B = Beginning; D = Developing; S = Secure

Use with Lesson 12.8.

483

Class Checklist

Class _____

Dates _____

Learning Goals

Children's Names

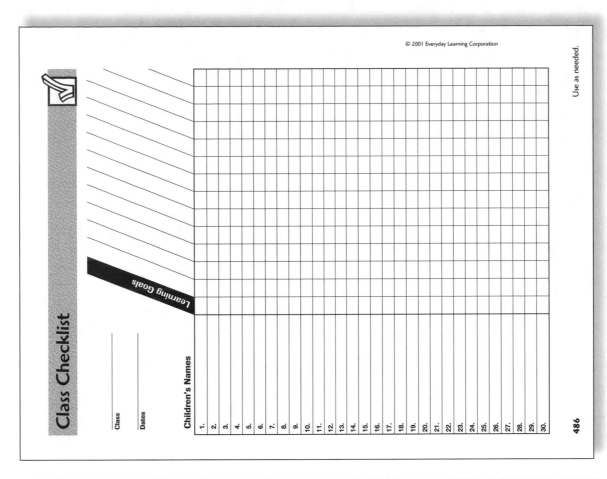

1.
2.
3.
4.
5.
6.
7.
8.
9.
10.
11.
12.
13.
14.
15.
16.
17.
18.
19.
20.
21.
22.
23.
24.
25.
26.
27.
28.
29.
30.

Use as needed.

486

Child's Name _____   Date _____

Individual Profile of Progress

Check ✔			Learning Goals	Comments
B	**D**	**S**		
			1.	
			2.	
			3.	
			4.	
			5.	
			6.	
			7.	
			8.	
			9.	
			10.	

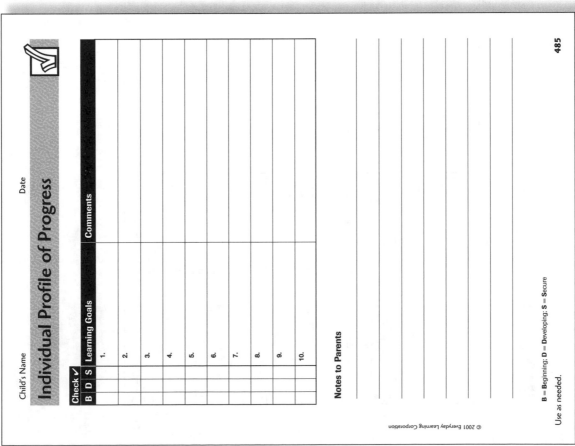

Notes to Parents

B = Beginning; **D** = Developing; **S** = Secure

Use as needed.

485

Class Progress Indicator

Mathematical Topic Being Assessed: _____

	BEGINNING	DEVELOPING OR DEVELOPING+	SECURE OR SECURE+
First Assessment After Lesson: _____ Dates included: _____ to _____			
Second Assessment After Lesson: _____ Dates included: _____ to _____			
Third Assessment After Lesson: _____ Dates included: _____ to _____			

Notes

Use as needed.

488

Names

Names

1.
2.
3.
4.
5.
6.
7.
8.
9.
10.
11.
12.
13.
14.
15.
16.
17.
18.
19.
20.
21.
22.
23.
24.
25.
26.
27.
28.
29.
30.

Names

1.
2.
3.
4.
5.
6.
7.
8.
9.
10.
11.
12.
13.
14.
15.
16.
17.
18.
19.
20.
21.
22.
23.
24.
25.
26.
27.
28.
29.
30.

Names

1.
2.
3.
4.
5.
6.
7.
8.
9.
10.
11.
12.
13.
14.
15.
16.
17.
18.
19.
20.
21.
22.
23.
24.
25.
26.
27.
28.
29.
30.

Use as needed.

487

Rubric

Beginning (B)

Developing (D)

Secure (S)

Use as needed.

490

Child's Name _____ Date _____

Parent Reflections

Use some of the following questions (or your own) and tell us how you see your child progressing in mathematics.

Do you see evidence of your child using mathematics at home?

What do you think are your child's strengths and challenges in mathematics?

Does your child demonstrate responsibility for completing Home Links?

What thoughts do you have about your child's progress in mathematics?

Use as needed.

489

Name _____ Date _____ Time _____

About My Math Class

Draw a face or write the words that show how you feel.

Good 😊 OK 😐 Not so good 🙁

1. This is how I feel about math:	**2.** This is how I feel about working with a partner or in a group:	**3.** This is how I feel about working by myself:
4. This is how I feel about solving number stories:	**5.** This is how I feel about doing Home Links with my family:	**6.** This is how I feel about finding new ways to solve problems:

Circle **yes**, **sometimes**, or **no**.

7. I like to figure things out. I am curious.

yes   sometimes   no

8. I keep trying even when I don't understand something right away.

yes   sometimes   no

Use as needed.

491

Name _____ Date _____ Time _____

About My Math Class

Circle the word that best describes how you feel.

1. I enjoy mathematics class.   yes   sometimes   no

2. I like to work with a partner or in a group. yes   sometimes   no

3. I like to work by myself.   yes   sometimes   no

4. I like to solve problems in mathematics.   yes   sometimes   no

5. I enjoy doing Home Links with my family.   yes   sometimes   no

6. In mathematics, I am good at _____

7. One thing I like about mathematics is _____

_____

8. One thing I find difficult in mathematics is _____

_____

Use as needed.

492

Name   Date   Time

Math Log B

Question:

Use as needed.

494

Name   Date   Time

Math Log A

What did you learn in mathematics this week?

Use as needed.

493

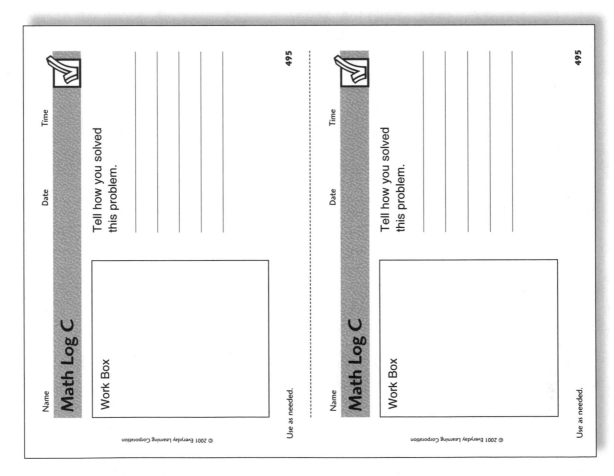

Name _____ Date _____ Time _____

Good Work!

:) I like this work because _____

© 2001 Everyday Learning Corporation

Use as needed.

496

Name _____ Date _____ Time _____

Math Log C

Work Box

Tell how you solved this problem.

495

Use as needed.

© 2001 Everyday Learning Corporation

Name _____ Date _____ Time _____

Math Log C

Work Box

Tell how you solved this problem.

495

Use as needed.

© 2001 Everyday Learning Corporation

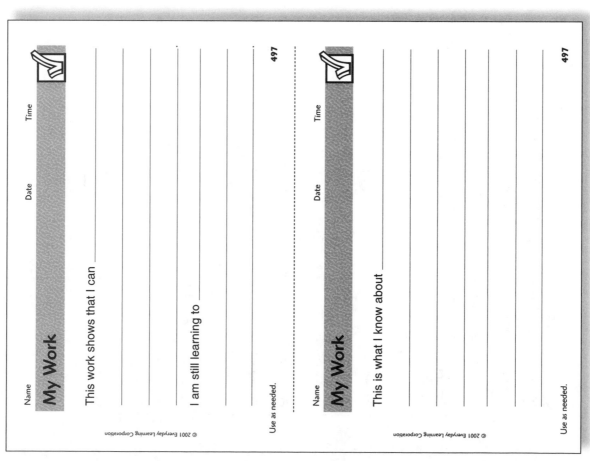

My Exit Slip

Name _____ Date _____ Time _____

Use as needed.

498

My Exit Slip

Name _____ Date _____ Time _____

Use as needed.

498

My Work

Name _____ Date _____ Time _____

This work shows that I can _____

_____

_____

I am still learning to _____

_____

Use as needed.

497

My Work

Name _____ Date _____ Time _____

This is what I know about _____

_____

_____

_____

_____

_____

Use as needed.

497

Geometry

© 2001 Everyday Learning Corporation

Name   Date   Time

1. Name 3 things in the classroom that look like a cube.

_____

_____

_____

2. Name 3 things in the classroom that look like a sphere.

_____

_____

_____

3. Name 3 things in the classroom that look like a cylinder.

_____

_____

_____

4. Name a shape found in the classroom. Draw it and tell what it is.

_____

_____

_____

Use as needed.

500

Name   Date   Time

Linear Measurement and Perimeter

Use your Pattern-Block Template. Trace these shapes: square, large hexagon, trapezoid, and one of the rhombuses. Measure and label each side of each shape. Then find the perimeters.

Square	Large Hexagon
Perimeter = _____ cm	Perimeter = _____ in.
Trapezoid	Rhombus
Perimeter = _____ in.	Perimeter = _____ cm

© 2001 Everyday Learning Corporation

Use as needed.

499

Glossary

assessment The gathering of information about children's progress. This information might include children's knowledge and use of mathematics, as well as their feelings about mathematics. The assessment is used to draw conclusions for individual and class instruction.

assessment sources Mathematical tasks or interactions that can be used for gathering data for assessment purposes.

concepts Basic mathematical ideas that are fundamental in guiding reasoning and problem solving in unfamiliar situations.

evaluation Judgments based on information gathered during assessment.

interviews Conversations between a teacher and individual children during which the teacher can obtain information useful for assessing mathematical progress.

kid-watching The observing and recording of children's interactions and communications during regular instructional activities.

long-term projects Mathematical activities that may require days, weeks, or months to complete.

Mathematics Interest Inventories A written format for assessing children's attitudes toward mathematics.

Math Logs Formats for developing written communication while gathering examples of children's mathematical thinking through writing, pictures, diagrams, and so on.

Ongoing Assessment The gathering of assessment data during regular instructional activities.

open-ended questions Questions that have multiple answers and ways of arriving at these answers. (Open-ended questions are good assessments for problem-solving and reasoning skills.)

outside tests School, district, state, or standardized tests. These tests may or may not match the curriculum.

performance The carrying out or completing of a mathematical activity that displays children's knowledge and judgment while they are engaged in the activity.

Periodic Assessment The more formal gathering of assessment information, often outside of regular instructional time. One example is end-of-unit assessment.

portfolio A sample collection of a child's mathematical work representing his or her progress over the school year.

Product Assessment Samples of children's work, including pictures, diagrams, or concrete representations.

progress The growth, development, and continuous improvement of children's mathematical abilities.

Progress Indicators A form upon which the results of sequential assessment tasks for various mathematical ideas, routines, and concepts can be recorded for the whole class during the school year, using such indicator categories as Beginning, Developing, and Secure.

reflective writing The ability to reflect and write about mathematics, on topics like accomplishments, confidence, feelings, understanding or lack of understanding, goals, and so on.

representative work A piece of work that represents a child's ability and that indicates progress made.

rubric A defined set of guidelines that gives direction for scoring assessment activities. The most useful rubrics are those derived from experience with a wide variety of performances of an assessment task.

self-assessment The ability of children to judge, reflect on, and acknowledge the quality of their mathematical thinking or productions.

standardized tests Typically, nationwide tests that are given, scored, and interpreted in a very consistent way, regardless of the population being tested.

validity of assessment The degree to which assessment data actually represent the knowledge, thought processes, and skills that children have attained.

Index